THE MAIDEN'S PRAYER

BY NICKY SILVER

★

★

DRAMATISTS
PLAY SERVICE
INC.

THE MAIDEN'S PRAYER

is dedicated to

Patricia Clarkson

THE MAIDEN'S PRAYER was produced by the Vineyard Theatre (Douglas Aibel, Artistic Director; Jon Nakagowa, Managing Director) in New York City, February 1998. It was directed by Evan Yionoulis; the set design was by Derek McLane; the costume design was by Jess Goldstein; the lighting design was by Donald Holder; the sound design and original music were by Mike Yionoulis; and the production stage manager was Shelly Bernstein. The cast was as follows:

Paul	Geoffrey Nauffts
Libby	Patricia Clarkson
Cynthia	Joanna Going
Taylor	Christopher C. Fuller
Andrew	Daniel Jenkins

The author wishes to extend his sincerest thanks to the following individuals and organizations: George Lane, David Warren, Peter Manning, Chuck Coggins, James Bart Upchurch III, Mark Meshurle, New York Stage and Film, Doug Aibel and the Vineyard Theatre, for providing me with an artistic home.

CHARACTERS

PAUL — Mid-thirties, well-mannered and attractive "in a book-ish, sort of way."

TAYLOR — Mid-thirties. Paul's best friend. He's down right "dashing." This, of course, is a rather fragile facade.

CYNTHIA — Mid-thirties. Taylor's wife. Quite beautiful. She has a charm and graciousness that borders on anachronistic.

LIBBY — Mid-thirties, Cynthia's slightly older sister. Also quite attractive, Libby is high-strung, and usually vulgar.

ANDREW — A man Paul picks up in Bloomingdale's. He is conscientiously cheerful.

GEORGE, ART — Other men Paul has dated. They are intended to be played by the actor playing Andrew.

THE MAIDEN'S PRAYER

ACT ONE

Scene 1

*In the darkness we hear Mendelssohn's "Wedding March."**
The lights come up on Paul. He is standing under a tree,
smoking a cigarette, dressed in a navy suit. We are in the back
yard of a rather grand house, facing the back door. He ad-
dresses the audience.

PAUL. I met Taylor when I was six years old. My family lived just over there — that was before my parent's divorce and my father's marriage to that *French* woman. I remember. He was playing tether ball — there used to be a tether ball court under this tree — by himself and as we'd just moved in my mother told me go and see if there were other children in the neighborhood so she could get "some work done for God's sake, get some of these boxes unpacked."

She used to say I "haunted" her. "Go outside and play, for God's sake. You're *haunting* me." As if I were a ghost, already dead and sent from beyond to torment her. I assume she meant this with affection.

The point is, I saw Taylor — I remember this perfectly — from my yard. He was blonder then, and it was a sunny day so his hair was very bright. At six years old I don't think I'd developed any real aesthetic, but I knew what drew my eye. So I crossed the yard and introduced myself. He forced me to play tether ball for a little while, but I was never athletic so I wasn't too happy. Then he showed me his toys, of which he had hundreds, mostly Curious George and Tin Tin dolls. His father was

---

* See Special Note on Songs and Recordings on copyright page.

a toy manufacturer and had the licenses. But I didn't care for Curious George, and I'd never heard of Tin Tin, so I convinced him to play *Dark Shadows*. *Dark Shadows* isn't a game it was a TV show, in case your unfamiliar, and it was very popular at that time. It was sort of a gothic horror soap opera focusing on the *century-spanning* love affair between the beautiful, if high-strung, Angelique, who was, by the way, a witch, and the object of her *unending* and unrequited love Barnibus Collins, who was a vampire.

So we played *Dark Shadows,* our version of playing "house" or "doctor," on Sunday afternoons unless it rained, in which case we went to the movies. Taylor was Barnibus, of course, and I was, it goes without saying, a perfect and thrilling Angelique. *(Libby bursts, overwrought, through the door. She's wearing a lavender bride's maid dress and carrying a bottle of champagne.)*

LIBBY.   Oh God!

PAUL.   What?

LIBBY.   I'm sorry.

PAUL.   What did you say?

LIBBY.   I didn't know anyone was out here.

PAUL.   I'm out here.

LIBBY.   Well, I see that. I thought it was still raining.

PAUL.   It's stopped.

LIBBY.   Thank God! I had to get out of there! I couldn't take another minute of the hypocrisy, the bone-chilling, grotesque hypocrisy! Everyone pretending everything is wonderful. Everybody feigning ignorance of the destruction and misery that's hanging in the air! It was making me sick — I'm not exaggerating — it was making me physically ill, keeping my face in a frozen expression of joy, when what I really wanted to do, with every molecule of my body, with every atom of my physical being, what I *really* wanted to do was smash this bottle on my table, number twelve, by the way, NEAR THE BACK, smash this goddamn bottle, lurch across the dance floor, leap onto my sister and cut out of her chest whatever malignant lump of mud is where her heart should be! *(She drinks from the bottle. Paul is embarrassed.)*

PAUL.   I don't believe we've met.

LIBBY. Oh, I'm sorry. I thought we had.

PAUL. I don't think so. I'm Paul. I'm a friend of Taylor's.

LIBBY. I'm Libby, S.O.B, which according to the wedding co-ordinator means sister of the bride. Do you have a cigarette? *(He gives her one.)* I keep meaning to quit, but I hardly think today is the day.

PAUL. *(Lighting her cigarette.)* Congratulations.

LIBBY. On what?

PAUL. Your sister's wedding.

LIBBY. Are you being ironic?

PAUL. I didn't think so.

LIBBY. You're a friend of Taylor's?

PAUL. Yes.

LIBBY. Pray for him.

PAUL. I don't understand.

LIBBY. You don't know my sister very well, do you?

PAUL. No. I've just met her a couple of times, but she seems awfully nice.

LIBBY. You're a bad judge of character.

PAUL. Taylor says she perfect, says she's wonderful.

LIBBY. Hmmmm.

PAUL. He loves her — and I'm glad.

LIBBY. Oh?

PAUL. I don't think I've ever seen him happy, really, before this.

LIBBY. Oh?

PAUL. No. You know, he was always restless and searching and, well, experimenting.

LIBBY. Experimenting?

PAUL. I don't want to speak out of turn.

LIBBY. You mean the drugs?

PAUL. Well —

LIBBY. You mean the drinking?

PAUL. I didn't think anyone knew.

LIBBY. We met in a support group.

PAUL. I don't think it was ever serious. He was just rebelling. Although I was worried, when his father died that he might go over the — but you know Taylor tells me Cynthia's given him

9

a whole new lease on life, a fresh outlook, a new beginning.

LIBBY.   Well, Taylor sees the best in people, some people — IN HER! Don't get me wrong, I adore him, I mean, I really couldn't have a higher opinion, but he has a blind spot, trust me, where Cynthia's concerned. Would you like to know about my sister?

PAUL.   I don't think so.

LIBBY.   When she was five years old she tried to kill me. I am not speaking euphemistically. She tried to murder me! In my sleep! In the dark of the night! She crept into my room, not making a sound and put a plastic bag over my head. I woke up screaming, panting, gasping for breath in the middle of the night.

PAUL.   Children play pranks.

LIBBY.   You are so naive.

PAUL.   They don't understand there are consequences.

LIBBY.   She understood. She always understood. She knew what she was doing and she knew what she was. I'm the one who was slow to catch on. My parents turned a blind eye and they still do. They think she's sweet — and speaking of *eyes,* what message was she sending when I came home from school, an innocent first grader who still believed the world was just, to find that all my dolls, my *favorite dolls* had had their eyes gouged out, *out of their heads,* with something jagged!? For months I found them, stray doll eyes that had rolled into corners and under dressers and — Oh, I could read you a litany of horrors!! An endless list of acts so hateful —

PAUL.   Please don't!

LIBBY.   What?

PAUL.   Look, I don't know you. I've just met you.

LIBBY.   I'm Libby —

PAUL.   I know — but I have to say you're making me very uncomfortable! My best friend, someone I dearly love, has just married your sister and I don't want to hear these ugly things. I mean, you're obviously upset and exploding in some kind of … well, a seizure of venom. I'd like to help you if I can, but I don't want hear these attacks. I don't want to encourage this ugliness on what ought to be a beautiful day. Now, if I can help you, if it'll help you to chat, that's fine. I'm happy to keep you company. But can we please change the subject!?

LIBBY. Oh ... well. Pardon me. *(There's a pause. She steps on her cigarette.)*

PAUL. I like your dress.

LIBBY. *(Livid.)* My sister's idea of a practical joke! *(Cynthia emerges from the house. She's wearing a wedding dress and is graciousness itself.)*

CYNTHIA. *(Sweetly.)* There you are!

LIBBY. *(Whispered to Paul.)* Don't say anything.

CYNTHIA. Why are you out here? I was looking everywhere for you. Did you two meet? Paul this is my sister. Libby, this is —

PAUL. *(Pleasant.)* We met.

CYNTHIA. Libby's in the fashion industry —

LIBBY. *(Bragging.)* I'm a buyer.

CYNTHIA. She buys buttons.

LIBBY. *(Correcting her.)* I buy *closure* for J Crew.

PAUL. Pardon me?

CYNTHIA. Isn't that buttons? That is buttons, isn't it?

LIBBY. And zippers. And ... buttons.

PAUL. That must be fun.

LIBBY. It's not.

CYNTHIA. *(To Paul.)* Why are you out here?

LIBBY. *(Proud.)* I wasn't feeling well.

PAUL. I'm so sorry I'm late with my gift —

LIBBY. I felt sick.

PAUL. I have one coming, I swear, it's just that —

LIBBY. Ill.

PAUL. I haven't picked it out.

CYNTHIA. *(To Libby.)* Are you better? Are you feeling —

LIBBY. Yes. Much. Thanks.

PAUL. I had one picked out, but then I decided I didn't like it so I returned it. And then I realized it didn't matter if *I* liked it —

CYNTHIA. Don't worry. I'm just glad you're here.

PAUL. Thank you.

CYNTHIA. Who knows when we'll see you.

PAUL. What do you mean?

CYNTHIA. Well, you're in the city and we'll be out here.

PAUL. You're staying here?

CYNTHIA. At least for now.

PAUL. I didn't know.

CYNTHIA. It's just sitting empty, since his father died, this beautiful house! Taylor took it off the market and took a second mortgage —

LIBBY. I don't want to talk right now. Don't pressure me. Please. Just don't make me say things! *(A brief awkward moment for Cynthia and Paul.)*

PAUL. Should I go in —

LIBBY. *(Rushing to him.)* Don't! If you stay we'll have a pleasant chat. We will. We'll talk about the wedding and the food and the weather —

CYNTHIA. Are you all right? *(Libby nods. Paul tries to salvage the moment.)*

PAUL. It really was a lovely ceremony.

CYNTHIA. Thank you. I'm so glad you're not angry about, you know, about not being the best man. I know it upset Taylor, a lot — the idea that you were upset. But we thought it was appropriate that my cousin — I don't know why. We never see each other. I'm just happy you're here. *(She kisses him on the cheek.)* Where's Allen?

PAUL. Allen?

CYNTHIA. Isn't that his name? The man you live with?

PAUL. Oh, he's gone.

CYNTHIA. He left?

PAUL. I mean I'm not seeing him.

CYNTHIA. I'm sorry.

PAUL. We weren't living together.

CYNTHIA. I'm so sorry.

PAUL. I brought George.

CYNTHIA. Well, good for you. Moving on.

PAUL. But he left.

CYNTHIA. I'm sorry?

PAUL. He went home.

CYNTHIA. So early?

PAUL.   Actually he got out of the car on the Long Island Expressway.

CYNTHIA.   I hope he's all right.

PAUL.   I'm sure he's fine.

CYNTHIA.   Did you call him?

PAUL.   I lost his number.

CYNTHIA.   Oh?

PAUL.   I just met him last night.

CYNTHIA.   I see.

PAUL.   In a bar. He was self-conscious about his outfit and de-cided not to come.

CYNTHIA.   That's just silly. He's *your* friend and we would've loved meeting him.

PAUL.   I tried to convince him, but he said he couldn't be comfortable in riding chaps. *(That image disturbs Cynthia.)*

LIBBY.   HOW CAN YOU STAND THERE AND MAKE SMALL TALK!!?

CYNTHIA.   What?

LIBBY.   I don't know why I'm surprised! Nothing you do should surprise me at this point!!

PAUL.   I think I should go —

LIBBY.   No, no. Excuse me — Don't leave us alone — I'll just stand quietly over here. By myself. Tell us more about the *cheap trick* you picked up last night.

CYNTHIA.   We should all go inside. I should throw the bouquet.

LIBBY.   You go ahead. I need some air.

PAUL.   I'll stay with her.

CYNTHIA.   Well, if you're sure you'll be along —

LIBBY.   Tell me why you did this!!

CYNTHIA.   What?

LIBBY.   Why the fuck did you do this?!

CYNTHIA.   Do what? What *is* the matter, Libby? If something's bothering you, I wish you would just tell me. I wish you could be open about it. We're sisters. We shouldn't be building walls, we should be able to communicate.

LIBBY.   You knew I was in love with Taylor so you seduced him and got knocked up!!

CYNTHIA. … Well. That's better. That's how sisters should talk.

LIBBY. You did it on purpose! You did it to hurt me!

PAUL. I'll be inside —

CYNTHIA. No, no. Stay.

PAUL. I really don't think —

CYNTHIA. Stay, Paul. You're Taylor's best friend and I wouldn't want you to leave with the wrong impression. You can't believe Libby's hysterical outburst —

LIBBY. I am not hysterical!

CYNTHIA. She's always been high-strung.

LIBBY. Do you deny it!?

CYNTHIA. Libby, I thought we were clear about this — My sister dated Taylor briefly, very briefly —

LIBBY. Three weeks! We dated for three weeks! Do you call that brief?

PAUL. I call it a lifetime.

CYNTHIA. That was last year. It was all dead and dust before I ever entered the picture.

LIBBY. You twist everything!

CYNTHIA. *(Concerned.)* Libby, are you seeing Dr. Porter?

LIBBY. No. No, as it happens, I'm not seeing Dr. Porter.

CYNTHIA. My sister's been in therapy, in and out of therapy, for a few years — Don't you think you should — continue seeing Dr. Porter?

LIBBY. Dr. Porter died, Cynthia.

CYNTHIA. Oh.

LIBBY. He died last summer. He had a heart attack and died.

CYNTHIA. Are you going to your meetings?

LIBBY. I don't have meetings. I don't go to meetings. Besides, I don't need Dr. Porter, or a support group or a twelve-step program to see what's obviously true. I don't need a psychologist to explain your malevolent machinations —

CYNTHIA. I don't want to hear anymore. This is my wedding day! I'm going to go inside and throw my bouquet. Are you coming or not?

LIBBY. No.

CYNTHIA. *(Fighting tears.)* Fine. But I have to tell you, Libby,

I'm — I am deeply hurt that you're trying to ruin this for me. I am horrified that you could be so selfish, so completely selfish, as to try to destroy what ought to be the most important day in my life. Whatever differences we've had, I never thought — *(Cynthia starts to cry as Taylor emerges from the house wearing a tuxedo. He is all good cheer.)*

TAYLOR. What's everyone doing out here?!

CYNTHIA, PAUL and LIBBY. *(They all turn away, embarrassed.)* Nothing.

TAYLOR. You're all missing it! Uncle Stan has lost his mind! He's singing with the band!

CYNTHIA. *(Hiding, still crying.)* Oh?

TAYLOR. I tried to stop him but the man is possessed. He's doing the entire score of *Three Penny Opera.*

PAUL. I better go, don't want to miss "The Ballad of Immoral Earnings!"

TAYLOR. No, wait, Paul.

PAUL. *(Defeated.)* Oh but I really think —

TAYLOR. I haven't had a minute with you. My best friend and we haven't said hello. You look great! *(The men embrace.)*

PAUL. So do you —

TAYLOR. I go to meetings once a week.

PAUL. *(Not sure how to respond.)* I'm sorry that I haven't sent a gift.

TAYLOR. What?

PAUL. I can't seem to decide on anything.

TAYLOR. Forget it.

PAUL. I looked in Tiffany's. I looked in Saks'.

TAYLOR. Don't worry.

PAUL. I looked in Bendel's and Bergdorf Goodman.

TAYLOR. It's all right.

LIBBY. No one cares that you haven't sent a gift! You have a year. Read Emily Post.

PAUL. Oh…. You know how happy I am for you.

TAYLOR. *(Looking at Cynthia, who is still weeping a bit, her back to the men.)* She's quite a woman.

PAUL. Certainly is.

TAYLOR. She's something else.

PAUL.   And then some.

TAYLOR.   I don't know where I'd be without her. Well, I do know where I'd be and I'm glad I'm not there. Where's Art?

PAUL.   Art?

TAYLOR.   Art.

PAUL.   I don't ...

TAYLOR.   Wasn't that his name? The man after Allen?

PAUL.   *(Thinking.)* After Allen?... No, no. Art was before. *Bart* was after. I brought George. He left. *(Cynthia makes a small whimpering sound.)*

TAYLOR.   Honey, what is it?

CYNTHIA.   Nothing. I'm just —

TAYLOR.   Something is wrong.

CYNTHIA.   It's just the emotion of the day.

TAYLOR.   You're sure?

CYNTHIA.   *(Nodding.)* Hmmmm.

TAYLOR.   *(Agitated.)* You shouldn't be crying. You shouldn't be upset. It can't be good for the baby. Did something happen? Did someone do something to you? Say something to you?

LIBBY.   Oh tell him! Tell him the truth! I don't care. You'll only tell him later! Behind my back you'll tell him *your version* of things, so I'd just as soon you tell him now, in front of me, so I can correct your inaccuracies!

TAYLOR.   Tell me what?

LIBBY.   Tonight you'll tell him I attacked you. You'll tell him I threw stones or something. So tell him with me here —

PAUL.   I really think I should —

CYNTHIA.   No, Paul stay! You saw the whole thing. You're an impartial observer.

PAUL.   But I don't want to stay!

LIBBY.   Let him go!

CYNTHIA.   Stay!

PAUL.   Please!

TAYLOR.   What happened! Will someone tell me what's going on!

PAUL.   Nothing very much. We were talking —

CYNTHIA.   My sister attacked me!

LIBBY.   Oh my God!

16

CYNTHIA. *(Near tears again.) With words,* words like daggers on my wedding day!

LIBBY. I don't feel like talking anymore. You all talk. I'll listen.

CYNTHIA. *(Turning away.)* She hates me!

TAYLOR. Libby, what did you say!? *(To Paul.)* What did she say?

PAUL. I wasn't listening.

LIBBY. What's the difference!? You've decided! You've decided who was right and who was wrong! You've already decided, so what's the difference?!! *(There is a long pause. Libby looks forward. Taylor and Cynthia look at her with pity. Paul could not feel more awkward.)*

PAUL. Cynthia says you'll be moving in here.

TAYLOR. Libby —

CYNTHIA. *(With real kindness.)* Don't be angry with her. I'm not. I'm trying to let it go.

TAYLOR. But —

CYNTHIA. You have to realize that this — would, naturally, be a frustrating day for Libby —

LIBBY. *(Quietly.)* Please.

CYNTHIA. *(Kneeling next to her.)* It's all right. I understand.

LIBBY. *(Under her breath.)* Don't.

CYNTHIA. You're upset. You're in love with Taylor. You've always been in love with Taylor. And you think I stole him from you, as if he were a ring or some kind of prize. But I didn't. You think because you love him that he has to love you. But he doesn't. I'm sorry. You have to face that. I'm not trying to hurt you, honestly. I'm trying to help. You have to get over whatever romantic ideas you have — you seem to think he's going to come to his senses or something. You think he'll wake up tomorrow and discover feelings for you. But he loves me. I *am* sorry, but you have to accept that. Tell her.

TAYLOR. *(Simply.)* It's true Libby. I'm sorry. I don't love you. That way. I love Cynthia. *(A moment passes. Libby is devastated but still.)*

CYNTHIA. We've been out here long enough. It's time to throw the bouquet.

TAYLOR. Let's go.

CYNTHIA. And I think I felt a drop. *(Cynthia and Taylor go to exit. Cynthia stops at the door.)* Are you coming? *(Libby nods. Cynthia exits.)*

PAUL. Are you all right?

LIBBY. I'm fine.

PAUL. Are you going in — try to catch the bouquet?

LIBBY. She'd aim for my eyes.

PAUL. Oh. Well, then … it was nice meeting you —

LIBBY. Let's get out of here! *(Blackout.)*

Scene 2

A light comes up on George. He wears leather riding chaps over jeans, a plaid shirt and a vest.

A pair of handcuffs dangle from a belt loop. He is lighted from one angle only.

GEORGE. I met Paul last night so I don't have any great insight to his character. We were in this bar, "Spurs." And I thought he was kinda sexy in a bookish sorta way. And we were looking at each other and then we went to his place. We had sex. Three times. And then I tried to go to sleep but he was talking, trying to get me to agree to go to this wedding the next day. It was important to him, his best friend, yadda yadda yadda, I dunno. And I don't remember what I said 'cause I had a lot to drink. And smoked some pot. And taken some X…. And I was tired. But in the morning, I thought he was giving me a lift home. I live in Queens, where I work at a Citibank. I'm a loan executive. Then I realized I was being kidnapped, dragged to his friend's wedding, I made him pull over. I mean it seemed sort of nuts, you know. Like I started thinking he might be crazy 'cause I don't think I said I'd go. I don't think I agreed. Anyway he pulled over, we exchanged numbers, had sex one more time, and I got out. *(The angle of the light shifts and*

George removes his chaps and vest, becoming, Art.)
ART.   I met Paul the night of that wedding, his friend's wedding. He was doing his laundry and he seemed depressed. *(Smiling, lewdly.)* I asked him if there was anything I could do. *(The angel of the light shifts. Art strips down to a tee shirt and boxers, becoming Andrew.)*
ANDREW.   I met Paul three months after the wedding. I work in Bloomingdale's, in the crystal department. He was looking for a gift and he mentioned that he'd been looking for three months. I showed him stemware and paperweights, but frankly, I couldn't concentrate because I was flirting with him and he was flirting with me and so I didn't sell him anything. But he asked when I got off. I refrained from making the obvious joke and told him nine o'clock. We went out to dinner: Chinese. I had General Tso chicken. And I know, looking at him, that Paul isn't the most beautiful man in the world. I mean I know he's nice looking, but he's not unbelievable, and yet, to me, there is something perfect about him. The curve of his nose. And his lips. And he kisses beautifully. And his skin feels good against mine. *(The house slides halfway off, revealing Paul's bedroom. It may be a sparse suggestion, but there needs to be a bed, a night table with a picture of Taylor on it, a door to the bathroom and an entrance. It is late at night. Paul is in bed. Andrew is looking out the window. Paul sits up and turns on the light.)*
PAUL.   What are you doing?
ANDREW.   You have a beautiful view.
PAUL.   What time is it?
ANDREW.   Is that Newark?
PAUL.   *(Apologetic.)* You should really go.
ANDREW.   It's early.
PAUL.   I'm sorry but —
ANDREW.   I was thinking —
PAUL.   I have to work in the morning.
ANDREW.   What do you do?
PAUL.   I write advertising copy.
ANDREW.   I want to stay.
PAUL.   I have to be there very early.
ANDREW.   I don't mean tonight.

PAUL. Good, because I have a meeting at nine.

ANDREW. I meant ... well, you have a big apartment and I have a tiny apartment —

PAUL. I have to get to sleep.

ANDREW. We both smoke. Although I haven't smoked in a few years. I'm still a smoker. I mean by nature. It wouldn't take much.

PAUL. It was very nice meeting you —

ANDREW. I find you very sexy.

PAUL. Thank you. But — I'm afraid I've forgotten your name.

ANDREW. It's Andrew.

PAUL. Thank you, Andrew. But I really have to get to sleep.

ANDREW. I want to move in.

PAUL. Where? Here? What?!

ANDREW. You have nice things and I really enjoyed the sex. You have that rare ability to be both tender and violent at the same time.

PAUL. I enjoyed it too but —

ANDREW. My apartment is decrepit and filthy.

PAUL. Clean it.

ANDREW. Don't you like me?

PAUL. I don't know you.

ANDREW. We've just had sex. Three times. We've been as intimate as human beings can be. I think I really care for you.

PAUL. I'm flattered, but —

ANDREW. Don't be so closed-minded. Happiness comes as a surprise.

PAUL. I really think you should go.

ANDREW. Happiness is a slippery proposition, Taylor.

PAUL. My name isn't Taylor.

ANDREW. What?

PAUL. My name is Paul.

ANDREW. You said you were Taylor.

PAUL. Be that as it may.

ANDREW. You made up your name?

PAUL. I did.

ANDREW. Why?

PAUL. Whim.

ANDREW. You lied to me?

PAUL. I did. So you see our relationship is based on deception. Now, I really have to get to sleep!

ANDREW. I love that about you. You're so creative! You're inventive. I adore you!

PAUL. Listen, Andrew —

ANDREW. Call me.... Anton!

PAUL. Why?

ANDREW. I always wanted to be an Anton.

PAUL. No.

ANDREW. *(Shrugging.)* All right.

PAUL. I'm sure your a very nice person. I'm sure you have many fine qualities —

ANDREW. Thank you.

PAUL. But I'm just not looking to be with someone right now. You understand that, don't you?

ANDREW. Not really.

PAUL. I don't want a relationship.

ANDREW. *(Cheerful.)* You should've thought about that before you picked me up.

PAUL. Maybe I should have, but that doesn't change the facts. Look, I didn't mean to mislead you —

ANDREW. You didn't. We never discussed it.

PAUL. I don't want to hurt your feelings —

ANDREW. You're so sweet. I could tell that about you right away. Do you have cable? We don't have cable. We only get channel two and sometimes we get channel four, but mostly that's snow.

PAUL. Please get dressed.

ANDREW. Do you get the premium channels or just basic cable — not that it matters to me, really. I'm just curious.

PAUL. I'm asking you to get dressed. Please get dressed and go! I have to get up at seven in the morning so I can be awake and alert for a meeting at nine.

ANDREW. The way you look, right at this moment, with the light from the moon. This is a moment of perfection. This is one of those moments you wait for all your life and then you curse yourself because you don't have a camera. Do you have a camera?

PAUL. No.

ANDREW. Then I'll photograph you with my mind. *(Andrew does so.)*

PAUL. Please leave!

ANDREW. You wouldn't even know I was here. I'm very neat. I don't normally throw my clothes on the floor, I was overcome with passion. I can be quiet when I have to be. We don't even have to speak.

PAUL. Then what's the point of moving in?

ANDREW. Sex. Sex is the point. And cable television.

PAUL. I wanted a vase! I wanted some stemware!

ANDREW. Don't deny you find me attractive —

PAUL. I find you attractive, but —

ANDREW. Thank you. I find you attractive. What do you like best about me?

PAUL. But I don't want a relationship! And if I did, it wouldn't be with you!

ANDREW. What are you saying?

PAUL. I'm saying "Get out!"

ANDREW. *(Sincere.)* I don't understand.

PAUL. *(Stern, not cruel.)* We met. We had sex. Now leave.

ANDREW. I don't follow.

PAUL. I don't want to see you again.

ANDREW. Did I do something wrong?

PAUL. I'm not interested in you. I don't enjoy saying cruel things but you put me in this position — Now don't try to see me. Don't try to call me, the number I gave you was wrong anyway. Please don't make me say any more. I feel guilty enough as it is. Just go. Please. *(Pause.)*

ANDREW. Can I use your bathroom?

PAUL. Yes! Fine! Use the bathroom.

ANDREW. Thank you. *(Andrew picks up his clothes and goes to the bathroom.)* You'll change your mind. *(He shuts the door. Across the stage, Cynthia, now five months pregnant, dressed in a peignoir, enters and walks onto the yard. She looks around, distraught. After a moment, Paul picks up a sock Andrew missed and goes to the bathroom door.)*

22

PAUL.   You forgot something. *(There is no response.)* Andrew, you forgot, you missed a sock. *(No response; Paul tries the knob, but it's locked.)* Andrew! Are you all right? What are you doing in there! Open the door!

ANDREW.   *(Offstage.)* I'm fine I'll be right out.

PAUL.   God!

ANDREW.   *(Offstage.)* You have a huge bathroom! *(Paul goes and sits on the bed. There is a shift in the light, suggesting a surreal quality, and Paul looks out and addresses the audience.)*

PAUL.   And while I waited for my Bartleby to leave the john, my mind wandered away from the specifics of my current predicament, absurd as it was. I was sort of rolling over, in my head, the vagaries of what we think is love. I started dreaming, wide awake, to my surprise. *(Taylor appears behind him, dressed in a suit.)*

TAYLOR.   I wish you could be happy for me.

PAUL.   I am.

TAYLOR.   You say that,

PAUL.   *(Turning to him.)* I am.

TAYLOR.   But I can tell.

PAUL.   *(After a beat.)* Oh.

TAYLOR.   Be happy for me.

PAUL.   Do you remember when we met? *(Taylor sits on the bed.)*

TAYLOR.   I was six.

PAUL.   The sun was in your hair.

TAYLOR.   I saw you walking towards me.

PAUL.   And I thought you had everything,

TAYLOR.   But I couldn't make you out.

PAUL.   And I didn't understand.

TAYLOR.   Because the sun was in my eyes.

PAUL.   Why you weren't happy.

TAYLOR.   I couldn't really see you.

PAUL.   You were never happy.

TAYLOR.   Are you?

PAUL.   I wanted, so much, to be the one to save you. *(They look at each other for a moment. In the distance, we hear a car. Cynthia responds to the sound by going to the door. Paul places his hand on Taylor's face and tenderly touches his lips.)*

23

CYNTHIA. *(Calling him.)* Taylor!?

TAYLOR. I have to go.

CYNTHIA. I'm out here!

TAYLOR. Cynthia's calling me. *(Taylor stands and exits. After a moment the lights in Paul's apartment return to normal. He looks at the bathroom, then goes to the door.)*

PAUL. Andrew. Andrew! You really have to leave!

ANDREW. *(Offstage.)* You have such classy soap! *(As Paul returns to his bed, across the stage Taylor joins Cynthia.)*

TAYLOR. There you are.

CYNTHIA. I thought you'd never get home. *(They kiss.)*

TAYLOR. I'm sorry.

CYNTHIA. You're late.

TAYLOR. Business.

CYNTHIA. Going better?

TAYLOR. Going fine. Don't think about it.

CYNTHIA. I'm sorry.

TAYLOR. For what?

CYNTHIA. It's my fault your worried, because it was my idea to live here. Now, the money is ...

TAYLOR. *(Kissing her.)* I wanted to.

CYNTHIA. I convinced you.

TAYLOR. I'm happy. Here. With you.

CYNTHIA. Hmmmm.

TAYLOR. When I think of how I was living, it wasn't that long ago, in that tiny apartment.

CYNTHIA. It was awful.

TAYLOR. Eating food, cold from the can.

CYNTHIA. I never understood that. You had a stove.

TAYLOR. Hair down to here, sitting in front of the TV every night in a fog. I can't imagine where I'd be if it weren't for you.

CYNTHIA. I can. Face down on a stained mattress in a bad motel.

TAYLOR. You saved me. I love you. *(He kisses her, then sits on the ground.)* And I love it here.

CYNTHIA. Really?

TAYLOR. I never noticed it was beautiful. I never really looked around.

CYNTHIA. It is.

TAYLOR. God, I hated it growing up. My father loved it, which is probably why I didn't. He loved this house. Knocked down what was here before and built it himself — before I was born, of course, but I heard the stories. All those bedrooms were for brothers and sisters that never got born. That was when he thought she loved him, my mother that is. When she was well-behaved and he could still pretend.

CYNTHIA. She didn't?

TAYLOR. She didn't. But when I was little she was quiet and played along. I guess it was hard, or frustrating, because gradually, she started to speak. Just tiny stabs at first, but then huge vicious, disorganized attacks. My father retaliated by getting smaller and smaller until you couldn't find him. But he did love this house. We used to have picnics right here and Dad would say, "This is perfect. Bury me here. I want to be buried right here when I die." And mother replied, "Why wait?"

CYNTHIA. Why did she marry him?

TAYLOR. Well, there's the mystery.... You shouldn't be up.

CYNTHIA. I was waiting.

TAYLOR. You shouldn't be out.

CYNTHIA. I want to talk to you.

TAYLOR. Without a robe, without a coat.

CYNTHIA. It's warm.

TAYLOR. It's chilly.

CYNTHIA. It's June.

TAYLOR. It can't be good for the baby.

CYNTHIA. The baby is fine.

TAYLOR. We can't be too careful.

CYNTHIA. The baby is perfect.

TAYLOR. You could catch cold.

CYNTHIA. Listen to me.

TAYLOR. Put this on. (*He gives her his jacket, which she puts over her shoulders.*)

CYNTHIA. I'm very worried.

TAYLOR. (*Agitated.*) That can't be good for the baby. You have to think of the baby. I have to think for you.

CYNTHIA. I spoke to Libby this morning.

25

TAYLOR. Oh?

CYNTHIA. You know she was fired —

TAYLOR. She got fired?

CYNTHIA. Three weeks ago. She started out as the catalogue coordinator, then they demoted her, to fabric, then buttons, then they fired her. And she hasn't found anything and I don't know what she's going to do.

TAYLOR. Has she looked?

CYNTHIA. I don't know. I assume she's looked. I assume she's not just sitting around, you know, feeling sorry for herself. But apparently, she hasn't found anything. I want you to help.

TAYLOR. Is she drinking?

CYNTHIA. Is she breathing?

TAYLOR. I wish she'd find her higher power. You should force her to a meeting.

CYNTHIA. Me?

TAYLOR. You should drag her.

CYNTHIA. I wouldn't know what to wear.

TAYLOR. You should insist.

CYNTHIA. I want you to give her a job.

TAYLOR. You really think that's a good idea?

CYNTHIA. I don't know what else to do! She forbid me to tell our parents. She won't take help from me! — And it has to be your idea. She'd never agree if she thought it was mine.

TAYLOR. I don't know. You know how she is.

CYNTHIA. How is she?

TAYLOR. She seems to have *feelings* for me.

CYNTHIA. Oh, she must be over that. That was nothing. That was a crush.

TAYLOR. It could be very uncomfortable.

CYNTHIA. She has no money! She has no savings! She must be panicked, although she didn't let on, you know how competitive she is with me.

TAYLOR. I'd have to discuss it —

CYNTHIA. *(Getting upset.)* I'm not asking you to just *give* her money. I'm not asking for charity.

TAYLOR. I don't know.

CYNTHIA. She's my sister!

TAYLOR.   What can she do? She has no training.

CYNTHIA.   Things. She can do lots of things, I'm sure. I'm sure she has many skills that have simply been … untapped. You don't have to find her a good job. You don't have to make her vice president or anything.

TAYLOR.   Thank God. *(Cynthia thinks for a moment; In Paul's apartment his intercom buzzes. He goes to it.)*

PAUL.   *(Into intercom.)* Who is it? *(Paul sighs and waits, still, by the door.)*

CYNTHIA.   She knows things. She knows buttons and zippers.

TAYLOR.   I just don't know what I can do.

CYNTHIA.   There must be something! Something you could find for her!! That's all I'm asking!! She needs me! She needs us!

TAYLOR.   Calm down. Don't get upset. Think of the baby.

CYNTHIA.   I'm going inside! *(She exits.)*

TAYLOR.   *(Calling after her.)* I'll do something. I will. *(He follows her. Paul opens his door revealing Libby, who is hysterical. She's wearing a raincoat, belted at the waste.)*

LIBBY.   I have to talk to you!

PAUL.   What are you doing here?

LIBBY.   The most horrible, humiliating thing has happened!

PAUL.   Could we talk tomorrow?

LIBBY.   No, no, no! We can't! I can't! It can't wait!

PAUL.   It's the middle of the night.

LIBBY.   It's not even two.

PAUL.   But I have a situation on my hands.

LIBBY.   I didn't want to mention this because you might think badly of me. But, Paul, you're my best friend. I didn't want to say anything — I didn't want to scare you off because I know being my best friend carries a lot of responsibility — do you have a cigarette?

PAUL.   *(Handing her one.)* I thought you were quitting?

LIBBY.   Today is not the day! — I know we've only known each other a few months but I don't make friends very easily. I don't know where to meet people. And tonight, I need a friend! *(She lights her cigarette.)*

PAUL.   Why? What's the matter? What —

LIBBY. I don't know how it happened! I don't know how *this* happened! To me!

PAUL. Calm down.

LIBBY. I can't calm down!! I can't stop shaking!

PAUL. Tell me what happened.

LIBBY. You'll judge me.

PAUL. I won't.

LIBBY. Everybody judges everybody.

PAUL. I don't.

LIBBY. Well, *I* judge everybody! It's human nature. It's unavoidable. I mean you try to be open-minded and not set yourself up as some kind of arbiter of morality, but I can't help it!

PAUL. What happened?!

LIBBY. Well, here goes. Here goes. As you may or may not have noticed I've been a little depressed lately.

PAUL. I noticed.

LIBBY. You did? How?

PAUL. The crying jags. The three A.M. phone calls. The continual drinking.

LIBBY. I had no idea I was so obvious — I have to be more stoic. I don't think it's good to just go flashing your feelings all over the place. — Anyway, I've been a little depressed, which I don't think is inappropriate. I don't think it's excessively neurotic or anything — Dr. Porter used to say not all depressive, phobic, self-destructive urges are neurotic. Sometimes it's *appropriate* to want to want to burn yourself with a cigarette — anyway, I thought I was dealing with the Taylor/Cynthia situation as well as could be expected.

PAUL. You drank too much, spent too much, cried too much and called in sick until you got fired.

LIBBY. Well, your expectations are unrealistically high.

PAUL. I'm just saying.

LIBBY. Your judging me aren't you?

PAUL. No.

LIBBY. I'm glad I got fired! I mean I hated that job. I really did. It was so degrading! Do you have any idea how exhausting it is to have to feign excitement over the renewed popularity of the TOGGLE BUTTON!! Just how small can a person's world shrink?! THE TOGGLE BUTTON, PAUL! So screw them! Fuck them! I don't need them! I don't need buttons and I don't need them! You will notice my raincoat has no buttons! I cut them off. I cut all the buttons off of everything I own in a cry of protest!!

PAUL.   What about the zippers?

LIBBY.   Well, I'm not insane. Anyway, I've looked for as job. I tried! I thought about it. — You have no idea of the kind of financial strain I'm under.

PAUL.   I said I'd lend you money.

LIBBY.   I couldn't take it.

PAUL.   I'm going to write a check.

LIBBY.   I'd tear it to confetti. I know myself. I'd never pay you back and then you'd hate me, or if you forgot, I'd remember and it would hang between us all the time, blocking my view. Where was I? Money, job, depressed, drinking — Yes! You were right last week when you told me I've been drinking too much. I realized that tonight when I ran out of alcohol. So I went to the liquor store and my card was declined.

PAUL.   What'd you do?

LIBBY.   Well, I thought, I'll do what Paul does. I'll anesthetize myself by having anonymous sex continually with a series of nameless, faceless strangers.

PAUL.   I don't do that —

LIBBY.   Oh wake up and smell the coffee. I'm not judging, by the way. It's my nature, yes, but in this instance what do I care if you fuck and suck your way to the hall of fame. Just as long as your safe. You are safe, aren't you?

PAUL.   Perfectly.

LIBBY.   So I put on my sexiest black dress and went to the bar on my corner. I thought it was tasteful. I thought I looked classy! *(She removes her raincoat revealing a black cocktail dress of dubious taste, in which she, indeed looks very sexy.)* Apparently I've lost touch with the popular aesthetic.

PAUL.   It's very ... nice.

LIBBY.   Can you believe I paid five hundred dollars for this dress? I had a job at the time. So, I'm sitting at the bar drinking my club soda, having turned over the leaf of sobriety, and

29

the seconds are dragging by like hours and no one talks to me. And I wish I were dead. I'm feeling sorry myself all over. I mean what do I have? Who do I have?

PAUL.   You have me.

LIBBY.   Well you're not enough!! I'm sorry, but we're friends and it would be different if I hadn't known Taylor, if I hadn't been in love, if I hadn't felt, really, the kind of love from novels, from Brontë novels and teenaged songs. But I did and now I just feel sick! I feel sick and full of some kind of poison all the time!!

PAUL.   What happened!?

LIBBY.   Well, I'm sitting at the bar, getting older and older, and then, finally, this guy, this older guy, he offers to buy me a drink. I think, jackpot, fabulous. So I have a stinger. Then another.... His name is Jack. He's gotta be sixty. And if he weighs an ounce he tips the scales at three bills. He's big. But he seems perfectly nice. and I'm glad to have the drink. And, believe it or not, I'm glad that he's talking and I don't have to be entertaining or charming or anything. I can just sit and drink and listen. He's divorced. Two kids. In the security business and I'm sure he's a nice person. I'm sure he's a perfectly fine human being ... but, um ... *(She's finding it difficult to talk.)* Eventually he asks me if I'll go back to his apartment. And I think of you, and I think of Taylor, and I don't really answer, I don't say anything. I just nod. His apartment is fine. All the furniture looks like it's rented. Everything matches like a room in a department store. There are pictures of his children on the bookcase. A boy and a girl who stare, smiling at us the whole time. And he takes off my coat and he's mumbling quietly that I'm beautiful ... and I'm trying to enjoy it ... because it's nice to be told. And we go to the bedroom and he loosens his tie and unzips my dress. He turns off the light so I can't see his body. And he puts his hand on my shoulder, which doesn't feel bad, moving my hair and kisses my collar bone, and then my breast, and makes sounds. And then he kisses my mouth and my eyes are closed so I'm somewhere else, with someone else, with Taylor. And then this man, this Jack, this divorced father of two puts me on the bed and climbs on top of me and we have sex ...

and the horrible thing of it is … I didn't mind. I didn't care. It wasn't pleasant or ugly or thrilling or awful. It was nothing. It was just … brief.

PAUL. Well —

LIBBY. And then he turned on the light. He grabbed his bathrobe and ran, afraid I would see him, into the bathroom. I got dressed. And when he came out he was dressed. "Do you want a ride home?" I nodded. And then, he walked towards me. And when he reached me he put one hand on my neck and pulled my head towards his until our lips touched. And while he kissed me, with his other hand, he found my hand, and he put, in my hand, three, folded, one hundred dollar bills…. And then he whispered thank you.

PAUL. Oh my God.

LIBBY. I wasn't, really, insulted.

PAUL. *(Holding her.)* Oh my God.

LIBBY. *(Crying.)* I was grateful.

PAUL. Oh my God.

LIBBY. I was grateful.

PAUL. It's okay.

LIBBY. I was glad for the money.

PAUL. Sssshhh.

LIBBY. I didn't want to go home. I told him I lived here.

PAUL. Good.

LIBBY. I'm sorry.

PAUL. No, no. You did the right thing.

LIBBY. I could've given it back. I could've stormed out. I could've … I could've …

PAUL. You were stunned. You didn't know what to do.

LIBBY. No. You don't understand. I was stunned, for a moment. Just a moment. And then I decided. Fine…. This is how I live.

PAUL. Oh.

LIBBY. This is how I live.

PAUL. It'll be fine.

LIBBY. Will it?

PAUL. Yes. Stay here tonight.

LIBBY. No —

PAUL. Please.

LIBBY. Thank you. Thank you, Paul. *(She kisses him sweetly.)*

PAUL. Just don't, you know, expect to earn too much.

LIBBY. Cocksucker.

PAUL. Stay here.

LIBBY. Can I wash my face?

PAUL. Of course. *(She stands and as she approaches the bathroom, the door opens by itself. She sees Andrew.)*

LIBBY. *(Small.)* Who is that?

PAUL. Oh. I forgot to tell you ... *(As she walks into the bathroom and the lights fade out on the scene.)*

Scene 3

Andrew, dressed in chinos and his tee shirt, steps into a pool of light and addresses the audience. He's cheerful.

ANDREW. I didn't mind it in the bathroom. Frankly, I'd made a pretty comfortable bed for myself. I lined the tub with Paul's towels and used his bathrobe as a pillow. I'd have been happy to stay there indefinitely: watching TV while he was at work, hiding when he wanted his privacy, and, when Paul got horny, we could have sex. But then Libby needed to use the toilet. I'd been listening to her story, so I thought she deserved her privacy. And I liked her right away, really, even before I saw her, while I was eavesdropping. I thought she had a rare poetic and fragile quality. *(A light comes up on Libby, who addresses the audience.)*

LIBBY. "Who the fuck is this?!" I thought to myself. *(Libby's light goes out.)*

ANDREW. So I left the bathroom. Paul tried to get me to leave while Libby peed. But I was smart and left my clothes in there, thinking he couldn't very well hurl me out onto the city streets in my underpants. Besides he didn't *really* want me to go. I could tell. And I was still unconvinced when, after Libby finished, he threw my clothes out the window. Some people don't know themselves very well and they fight happiness tooth

32

and nail. I said I didn't care about those clothes. They were old clothes and I hoped a homeless person found them and put them to good use. He was angry and started to call the police. It was Libby who convinced him not to. So the three of us chatted. And then after a while we played Risk, the game of world domination. I won. Then Paul fell asleep. Then Libby fell asleep. And I went back to the tub. He was gone when I woke up and Libby found this pair of chinos in his dresser. I love them. I love the way they feel and smell and fit. I love everything about them. I may never take them off. (*His light goes out as Libby's returns.*)

LIBBY.   Over the next three months I saw Jack, divorced father of two, once a week. The third time I saw him he asked if I would be interested in seeing a friend of his. So he introduced to me Leonard, married father of one, who introduced me to Arthur, whose marital status never came up. (*Blackout.*)

Scene 4

> *The house slides back to its original position. It's a sunny afternoon. Cynthia, who is now eight months pregnant, is standing under a tree. Paul is seated in a chair, a porch chair or an Adirondacks. There are also a couple of empty chairs and the makings of a tricycle on the lawn. Everyone is cheerful.*

PAUL.   But he *didn't* rob me.
CYNTHIA.   Still.
PAUL.   He was harmless. (*Taylor enters bringing them drinks.*)
TAYLOR.   Here you go.
CYNTHIA.   Thank you dear.
PAUL.   Have you picked a name?
TAYLOR.   Jeffrey.
PAUL.   You must be so excited.
TAYLOR.   Did you see the nursery?
PAUL.   I did —
CYNTHIA.   Did you hear this, Taylor?

TAYLOR. Hear what? — You shouldn't be standing. *(Taylor sits on the ground and tries to assemble the tricycle. His attention is often split.)*

CYNTHIA. Did you hear about this lunatic who locked himself in Paul's bathroom?

TAYLOR. I heard. I wish you'd sit down.

CYNTHIA. I don't want to sit down.

TAYLOR. But —

CYNTHIA. I'm pregnant, not sick. I'm fine.

TAYLOR. You'd be comfortable.

CYNTHIA. *(Just the slightest edge.)* There's a chair. If I wanted to sit I'd be in it. I don't want to sit.

TAYLOR. I'm sorry.

PAUL. Why Jeffrey?

TAYLOR. I can't remember.

CYNTHIA. And this man was there when you got home? The next night, after work, he was there?

PAUL. Yes. But it was all right. He's all right. He'd cooked dinner.

CYNTHIA. My God.

PAUL. Pasta primavera and fresh garlic bread.

TAYLOR. Honey why *did* we settle on Jeffrey?

CYNTHIA. What do you mean it was all right? The man was obviously deranged. I'm very worried about you.

PAUL. Worried about me?

TAYLOR. How did we come up with Jeffrey? I don't know any Jeffreys.

CYNTHIA. It's for my grandfather.

TAYLOR. His name was Joseph.

CYNTHIA. My other grandfather.

TAYLOR. His name was John.

CYNTHIA. It's the initial. It's the first letter. That way everybody's happy.

TAYLOR. *My* grandfather's name was Fred.

CYNTHIA. Almost everybody.

PAUL. I dated a Jeffrey once.

TAYLOR. *(Teasing.)* I bet you did.

PAUL. And a Joseph and a John. No Fred.

CYNTHIA. He could have killed you!

PAUL. Who?

CYNTHIA. This man. This man who wouldn't leave. He could have been a thief. He could have been an ax murderer.

PAUL. He worked in Bloomingdales. And I don't think they'd have an ax murderer in the crystal department.

CYNTHIA. Well in what department would they have one?

TAYLOR. *(To Cynthia.)* Are you chilly?

CYNTHIA. Sporting goods?

PAUL. Don't they test people who work in department stores. I saw something on television. They run some kind of personality test.

TAYLOR. I think I saw that.

CYNTHIA. People snap. They snap all the time. Perfectly nice people one day. The next day they open fire.

TAYLOR. Should I get you a sweater?

CYNTHIA. *(Sweetly.)* I'm fine, Taylor. I have a voice. If I'm cold, dear, I'll ask for a sweater.

TAYLOR. I'm sorry.

CYNTHIA. He's so over protective.

TAYLOR. I love you.

CYNTHIA. *(Sweetly.)* I know you do. But it's enough. All right? It's enough already.

TAYLOR. She gets cranky.

CYNTHIA. I'm not cranky.

TAYLOR. It's understandable.

PAUL. Naturally.

TAYLOR. The hormones and the weight.

CYNTHIA. I am not cranky.

TAYLOR. The other night I woke up and she was sitting on the floor, in the dark, with her pillow, or what was left of her pillow, in front of her and a scissors in her hand. She'd attacked the pillow, hacked it to bits.

CYNTHIA. The feathers kept sticking me.

TAYLOR. She just attacked it like a wild animal.

CYNTHIA. I got frustrated. I couldn't sleep.

TAYLOR. It was the funniest thing I ever saw!

CYNTHIA. It was not.

TAYLOR.   You should have seen her, like a savage! Stabbing away over and over again in a rage. It was a riot!

CYNTHIA.   It wasn't that funny.

TAYLOR.   It killed me.

CYNTHIA.   That's because you never lose your temper.

TAYLOR.   Yes I do.

CYNTHIA.   He never does.

TAYLOR.   Of course I do. Everyone does.

CYNTHIA.   *You* don't.

PAUL.   I think I've seen it. Not very often, but I think I've seen it.

CYNTHIA.   *(Slightly offended.)* Oh.

PAUL.   *(Embarrassed.)* Not very often.

CYNTHIA.   So anyway, what happened? How did you get rid of him?

PAUL.   I moved.

CYNTHIA.   What?

PAUL.   I'm in a new place.

CYNTHIA.   You're lying!

PAUL.   It was time anyway.

TAYLOR.   You were talking about moving.

PAUL.   I never liked that apartment.

CYNTHIA.   You moved!? Out of your home?

PAUL.   That was really my out-of-college apartment. I never intended to stay there all these years.

CYNTHIA.   So he could still be there, waiting for you to get home, for all you know!

PAUL.   I'm sure whoever rented it threw him out.

CYNTHIA.   I'm very worried.

TAYLOR.   Don't worry honey.

CYNTHIA.   I'm worried about Paul.

TAYLOR.   Oh.

PAUL.   I'm fine.

CYNTHIA.   You need to settle down. Don't we know anyone to fix him up with?

TAYLOR.   Thinking.

PAUL.   I don't want to settle down.

CYNTHIA.   You can't go on like this.

PAUL. Why not?

CYNTHIA. It's dangerous! You were lucky this time, that this, this —

PAUL. Andrew.

CYNTHIA. This Andrew didn't have a knife or a gun.

TAYLOR. What about Stanley Short in the shipping department?

CYNTHIA. God no. Horrible.

TAYLOR. He's nice.

CYNTHIA. He's *so* fat! We can't fix Paul up with a fat person.

TAYLOR. He's not that fat.

CYNTHIA. He's porcine. If they lived together Paul would starve to death! — You were lucky this Andrew didn't cut your throat!

PAUL. He didn't want to hurt me. He was in love with me.

CYNTHIA. Well, that's just lunatic.

PAUL. Pardon?

TAYLOR. What about Steve Peters?

CYNTHIA. Isn't he blind?

TAYLOR. So?

CYNTHIA. We don't want to saddle poor Paul with some blind person. What kind of life is that? Picking his clothes and reading menus out loud in restaurants for the rest of his life?

TAYLOR. He's very nice. He's a nice man.

CYNTHIA. No. No blind people for our Paul.

PAUL. You think only a lunatic could love me?

CYNTHIA. That's not what I meant.

TAYLOR. I love you.

CYNTHIA. We're talking about *romantic* love.

PAUL. You think only the deranged could fall "in love" with me.

CYNTHIA. Of course not. But this, this Andrew —

PAUL. You don't have to refer to him as "this" Andrew, I'll know who you mean.

CYNTHIA. He didn't even know you. It's falling in love with someone you don't know that's insane.

PAUL. Well, I thought so at first —

TAYLOR. Sean Eddings?

37

CYNTHIA. Limbless. The man is limbless.

PAUL. It was actually Libby who changed my mind.

TAYLOR. Libby?

CYNTHIA. I didn't realize you two had gotten so friendly.

PAUL. We have.

CYNTHIA. That's good. She needs a friend.

PAUL. We discussed it. And we decided —

TAYLOR. Philip Hunter!

CYNTHIA. Dead.

TAYLOR. Sorry.

PAUL. We decided —

TAYLOR. *(Disturbed.)* How'd he die?

CYNTHIA. Suicide, I think. You were saying?

PAUL. People fall in love with their *idea* of who someone is.

CYNTHIA. Well there's a piece of eighty-proof wisdom.

TAYLOR. He seemed so cheerful.

CYNTHIA. Who?

TAYLOR. Philip Hunter.

CYNTHIA. Oh.

TAYLOR. He used to whistle all the time.

PAUL. I remember him. He was at the wedding.

TAYLOR. So you met him?

PAUL. He was attractive.

TAYLOR. He'd have been perfect for you —

CYNTHIA. If he hadn't killed himself.

TAYLOR. You reject everyone.

CYNTHIA. We should fix him up with someone living.

LIBBY. *(Offstage.)* Hello!

TAYLOR. We're back here!

CYNTHIA. *(To Taylor.)* Now remember, it was your idea.

TAYLOR. She'd be happy if —

PAUL. What's going on?

CYNTHIA. Nothing. *(Libby enters in a simple, but elegant, navy dress.)*

LIBBY. What're you doing out here?

CYNTHIA. Isn't it nice!? *(Cynthia kisses Libby on the cheek.)*

LIBBY. It's hot.

TAYLOR. Do you think it's too hot?

LIBBY.   Hello Taylor. You look well.

TAYLOR.   I've been exercising and going to my meetings. You should try it.

LIBBY.   I detest exercise.

TAYLOR.   I meant the meetings.

LIBBY.   I assumed.

TAYLOR.   They've made Thursdays singles night. You should go. You might meet someone.

CYNTHIA.   What kind of drunken social outcast would she meet at one of those meetings?

LIBBY.   That's where I met Taylor.

PAUL.   *(Saving the moment.)* I think it's nice to get out of the city and see the clouds.

LIBBY.   *(Sitting on the arm of Paul's chair.)* How you lie.

CYNTHIA.   Well, look at that. You two could be a couple. You look adorable together.

LIBBY.   He's gay, Cynthia. But thank you for thinking of me.

CYNTHIA.   I know that. I'm kidding.

PAUL.   They're trying to fix me up.

LIBBY.   They need a hobby.

CYNTHIA.   Would you like a drink? Iced tea?

TAYLOR.   We're having salmon.

LIBBY.   *(Lighting a cigarette.)* No thank you. What's the deal? Why am I here?

CYNTHIA.   We'll all have lunch.

LIBBY.   You never invite me.

CYNTHIA.   Your phone's out of order.

LIBBY.   I changed my number.

TAYLOR.   Libby, we don't smoke.

LIBBY.   So?

TAYLOR.   I mean we don't smoke around Cynthia.

LIBBY.   We don't?

TAYLOR.   Because of the baby.

LIBBY.   We're outdoors.

CYNTHIA.   I would appreciate it.

LIBBY.   There is an endless expanse of sky to absorb the tar and nicotine. It's not going to affect the baby.

CYNTHIA.   Fine.

LIBBY. *(Pouting.)* I'll put it out.

CYNTHIA. Thank you.

TAYLOR. Gregory Lipton!

CYNTHIA. What about Gregory Lipton?

TAYLOR. For Paul.

CYNTHIA. You're still on that?

TAYLOR. Don't you think?

CYNTHIA. Actually he's not bad.

LIBBY. He's straight.

TAYLOR. He is?

LIBBY. Yes.

CYNTHIA. He is not.

TAYLOR. I always thought —

CYNTHIA. Gregory Lipton is gay.

TAYLOR. I assumed.

CYNTHIA. He's very effeminate.

LIBBY. Straight.

CYNTHIA. You don't know.

LIBBY. Straight!

CYNTHIA. You don't know that! How could you know that? He was my boyfriend. You only met him once or twice, I think I'd be in a much better position to figure out whether the man is gay or straight. I spent lots of time with him. I went places with him. I did things with him.

LIBBY. I fucked him!

TAYLOR. *(After a beat.)* Oh.

CYNTHIA. Well that doesn't prove anything.

LIBBY. Thank you.

CYNTHIA. You could easily have been an experiment or an aberration —

LIBBY. The first time could have been an experiment, I assume. But I fucked him a lot. I fucked him for a year. I fucked him twice a week the whole year you two were dating. When do we eat?

CYNTHIA. In a bit. We have something to tell you that I think is going to make you very happy.

LIBBY. Oh?

CYNTHIA. Yes.

LIBBY. I can't imagine.

CYNTHIA. Taylor and I were in bed the other night —

LIBBY. That's not it, is it?

PAUL. Ssshh.

LIBBY. Sorry.

CYNTHIA. And I was saying that I was worried about you.

LIBBY. You needn't be.

CYNTHIA. It's been four months. You've been unemployed for four months now. Are you aware of that?

LIBBY. Vaguely.

CYNTHIA. I know how hard things must be.

TAYLOR. And then I came up with the idea.

CYNTHIA. He did.

TAYLOR. Why don't you come to work for me?

LIBBY. What?

TAYLOR. For the company.

LIBBY. Oh. *(Libby stands to think about this.)*

CYNTHIA. Isn't that wonderful?

TAYLOR. You could start right away.

CYNTHIA. How generous is this man?

TAYLOR. I'm just sorry I didn't think of it sooner.

CYNTHIA. Nobody's perfect.

TAYLOR. What do you think?

CYNTHIA. It's not your field, we realize that.

TAYLOR. You could start on Monday.

CYNTHIA. But it's something.

TAYLOR. You can start tomorrow.

CYNTHIA. What do you say?

LIBBY. Paul, didn't you tell me, that Taylor told you things weren't going well?

PAUL. I may have.

CYNTHIA. *(To Taylor.)* You told Paul things weren't going well?

LIBBY. I thought business was bad. I thought you were laying people off?

CYNTHIA. *(To Taylor.)* You told Paul that?

TAYLOR. I don't remember,

LIBBY. *(To Paul.)* That's what you said.

41

CYNTHIA. Things are fine.

LIBBY. Oh?

CYNTHIA. Taylor exaggerates.

TAYLOR. Things have been much better lately.

PAUL. It *was* months ago.

LIBBY. How many people work at your office?

TAYLOR. Six.

LIBBY. There used to be eight?

TAYLOR. That's right. *(Libby thinks for a long moment.)*

LIBBY. What's my job?

TAYLOR. It's flexible.

LIBBY. I don't know anything about your business.

TAYLOR. We'll train you.

LIBBY. I don't know anything about manufacturing or toys.

CYNTHIA. I don't understand why you're not thrilled.

LIBBY. What's the job?

CYNTHIA. You should be thrilled!

LIBBY. Well?

CYNTHIA. You should be grateful.

LIBBY. What are my duties?

TAYLOR. We'll play it by ear.

LIBBY. You must've thought about it. What exactly do I do?

CYNTHIA. *(Irritated.)* Well, what can you do!?

LIBBY. I can do a lot of things.

CYNTHIA. You should just say yes and find out when you get there.

LIBBY. *(In control.)* That's what you'd like?

CYNTHIA. Paul, should she say yes?!

PAUL. I don't know.

LIBBY. I'm asking the details. That's all. Taylor's made me an offer and I want to find out some of the details.

CYNTHIA. What could they matter!?

LIBBY. Let's say I'm curious, all right? Let's just say I'm curious!

CYNTHIA. *(Snapping.)* Out of the goodness of his heart, Taylor, is offering you a lifeline! Taylor, who owes you *nothing*, is creating a job out of thin air because you're in trouble! And you want to know *exactly* what your duties are!! You have the gall to stand there and question him?! What kind of human being are you!? HOW DARE YOU!? You've never accomplished anything! YOU'VE NEVER ACHIEVED ANYTHING! YOU PISS YOUR LIFE AWAY, AND THEN, WHEN SOMEONE REACHES OUT, WHEN SOMEONE TRIES TO HELP YOU —

TAYLOR. Calm down!

CYNTHIA. WHAT'S THE DIFFERENCE?! WHAT'S THE DIFFERENCE IF IT'S MAKING COFFEE!?

LIBBY. Is that it?

CYNTHIA. IF IT'S EMPTYING GARBAGE CANS!!?

LIBBY. Is *that* it?

CYNTHIA. WHAT IS THE DIFFERENCE?!!

LIBBY. *(After a beat.)* This wasn't your idea, was it Taylor?

CYNTHIA. IT WAS!

LIBBY. *(Pause, near tears.)* Was it? *(There is a pause. The women watch him.)* It's all right. You don't have to answer.

TAYLOR. *(To Cynthia.)* I think you should lie down.

LIBBY. *(To Cynthia.)* It was your idea, wasn't it?

PAUL. I don't understand.

CYNTHIA. *(Attempting charm.)* I know how you are. I knew you wouldn't take the job if you thought I suggested it.

TAYLOR. She only wanted to help.

CYNTHIA. I know things are difficult.

LIBBY. *(To Taylor.)* You think so?

CYNTHIA. I wanted to help.

LIBBY. By putting me next to Taylor?

CYNTHIA. That wasn't the point.

LIBBY. By emptying garbage cans. By making coffee. By putting me next to Taylor, knowing how I feel —

TAYLOR. We assumed that was over —

CYNTHIA. *(Overlapping.)* You're not still holding onto that are you?

LIBBY. Knowing how I feel. That's what you wanted, isn't it!? You wanted me to have to face it every day —

CYNTHIA. Don't be silly.

PAUL. Maybe she thought —

LIBBY. Don't you understand? That was the idea! Day after day, knowing he was hers, knowing I was nothing, knowing how

43

I felt, knowing how I feel, knowing all of that — that I would go, *day after day* — this is how *smug* she is, how *unthreatened* she is by me — that I could go, day after day and feel my failure — I would go, day after day, and feel you, Taylor, close to me, and not wanting me. *(To Cynthia.)* Until *what?* UNTIL I DIED, CYNTHIA? UNTIL WHAT?

CYNTHIA. *(Simple.)* I wanted to help.

LIBBY. I don't want your help. I don't need your help. I don't need your charity or your money. I do very well.

PAUL. Libby —

CYNTHIA. How could you possibly —

LIBBY. Do you know what I do for a living? Do you? I'm a prostitute.

CYNTHIA. God.

LIBBY. Your sister is a prostitute!

TAYLOR. *(Chuckling, thinking she's kidding.)* Libby.

LIBBY. I have sex! Stone cold sober! Sex with businessmen who pay me because they can pretend I like them because I can remember their names. I'm a prostitute! *(Cynthia slaps her and exits.)*

TAYLOR. *(After a beat.)* How could you?

LIBBY. It's easy. I pretend they're you.

TAYLOR. How could you upset her?

LIBBY. Oh. *(Taylor exits.)*

PAUL. You know, I think you have just fucked us out of lunch.

LIBBY. *(Shrugging.)* She's a bad cook.

PAUL. I miss Andrew.

LIBBY. You do?

PAUL. I miss the dinners. *(Blackout.)*

Scene 5

A pool of light comes up on Cynthia, wearing a simple black dress, no longer pregnant. She addresses the audience, sweetly.

CYNTHIA. I keep thinking that I heard him cry. I keep thinking that I saw him. But I was unconscious. I was sleeping, float-

44

ing, flying over the house. Holding Jeffrey so he wouldn't fall. He has blond hair and he isn't crying. He isn't afraid. He knows I have him. He has tiny hands and one of them is touching me, on my chin, reaching up. He has blue eyes. I keep thinking that I had him, that I heard him. But I was unconscious. And when I woke up, Dr. Allen, who is the sweetest man, told me, that he was gone. That he ... had died. *(Slowly the lights come up. The house is gone. The stage is bare. Taylor is standing near her. Paul and Libby are also there, but not so close by. Cynthia continues to look straight out.)*

TAYLOR. You should lie down.

CYNTHIA. I'm fine.

TAYLOR. You need to sleep.

CYNTHIA. I'm fine.

TAYLOR. You need to eat.

CYNTHIA. I'm fine.

TAYLOR. *(After a pause.)* Let me hold you.

CYNTHIA. I'm fine.

TAYLOR. Let me help you.

CYNTHIA. I'm fine.

TAYLOR. Please.

CYNTHIA. I'm fine.

TAYLOR. Please.

CYNTHIA. *(A wail of pain.)* I'M FINE! I'M FINE! I'M FINE! I'M FINE! I'M FINE! I'M FINE *(Taylor makes a small move towards her, but she rushes away and falls to her knees. The other three watch as she weeps. After a moment it is Libby who walks to her and, kneeling with her, wraps her arms around her sister and rocks her slowly.)*

LIBBY. Ssshhhh. *(The lights fade out.)*

END OF ACT ONE

ACT TWO

Scene 1

The lights come up on the yard and the back of the house. Taylor is seated on the grass, trying to assemble the tricycle. Cynthia appears in the doorway. Her composure is firmly in place.

CYNTHIA.   What are you doing?
TAYLOR.   Do you know that there are no words on these instructions?
CYNTHIA.   What?
TAYLOR.   There are no words, just drawings with letters and arrows. This piece slides into that piece, slides into this piece, slides into that piece. It's a nightmare. Who do they think is putting these things together?
CYNTHIA.   What are you doing?
TAYLOR.   Trying to finish the tricycle.
CYNTHIA.   Why?
TAYLOR.   It's no use like this.
CYNTHIA.   But there's no one to ride it. *I'm* too big to ride it.
TAYLOR.   I know that.
CYNTHIA.   You're too big to ride it.
TAYLOR.   I realize.
CYNTHIA.   Why are you making it?
TAYLOR.   Cynthia — PAUSE
CYNTHIA.   Do you think it's going to rain?
TAYLOR.   Don't you want to try again?
CYNTHIA.   Try what?
TAYLOR.   It's been four months.
CYNTHIA.   I just don't understand why you're putting that thing together. You should take it back.
TAYLOR.   Months have passed.
CYNTHIA.   I bet they'd take it back anyway. I bet they would, if you told them what happened.
TAYLOR.   Why would I do that?

46

CYNTHIA.   So they'd take it back. Am I speaking Chinese?

TAYLOR.   Cynthia —

CYNTHIA.   *(Disturbed.)* You use my name to much.

TAYLOR.   I want a child.

CYNTHIA.   Can we talk about something else? I was reading a magazine the other day, or maybe it was a book, it was all about these people, I can't remember the details. Did you read it? *Sit*

TAYLOR.   I want a child. Don't you?

CYNTHIA.   *(Correcting him.) Another* child.

TAYLOR.   All right. *UP*

CYNTHIA.   Don't pretend things didn't happen. Things happened.

TAYLOR.   I know they did.

CYNTHIA.   Opportunities get missed.

TAYLOR.   Why don't we don't make love anymore?

CYNTHIA.   We make love.

TAYLOR.   We haven't.

CYNTHIA.   Don't be silly.

TAYLOR.   Not since way before —

CYNTHIA.   We make love all the time. Why just last night — that wasn't you? I'm sorry. — I'm just kidding.

TAYLOR.   We should make love. *TO HER — KNEELING*

CYNTHIA.   We make love. We do. Just not that often.

TAYLOR.   It's been four months.

CYNTHIA.   I know. You said that.

TAYLOR.   I want to hold you.

CYNTHIA.   I want to go away.

TAYLOR.   I want to taste you.

CYNTHIA.   I want to go to London. *America*

TAYLOR.   I want to be inside of you.

UP CYNTHIA.   Have you ever been to London? *New York*

TAYLOR.   No —

CYNTHIA.   When I was a little girl my father took me to London. *there* I loved it. All the money is different colors. It's wonderful!

TAYLOR.   I want to make love to you.

CYNTHIA.   *(Snapping.)* Well, you have to understand! You just have to understand. And wait!

TAYLOR.   *(After a beat.)* Maybe you should talk to someone.

47

CYNTHIA. *(Pleasant again.)* I spoke to *Libby* today. She called. She called to check up on me, to see "how I'm doing." It's so insulting.

TAYLOR. I meant a professional.

CYNTHIA. Libby's a professional. She's a prostitute.

TAYLOR. You know what I mean.

CYNTHIA. And I think prostitutes have to be very good listeners. That's what they say, on all the talk shows. The men come to them and pour their troubles out, all over the bed. And the whores have be very sympathetic, and understanding and good listeners. I'm sure it helps if they're good lays too.

TAYLOR. Fine.

CYNTHIA. I'm sorry.

TAYLOR. Would you like to go to London?

CYNTHIA. You don't want to go to London?

TAYLOR. Maybe we should.

CYNTHIA. We can't afford to go to London.

TAYLOR. We should get away.

CYNTHIA. Don't give in to me.

TAYLOR. What do you want!?

CYNTHIA. You know what I want!!

TAYLOR. … Oh.

CYNTHIA. I never even saw him. *(There is a long pause. They just look at each other. He returns to his work.)*

TAYLOR. The instructions don't have any words so I can't be sure I'm looking at this right side up. *(She starts to leaves, but stops at the door.)*

CYNTHIA. *(Softly.)* Don't you ever want to hit me? *(He turns around, shocked by her question, but she is gone. The light fades out.)*

Scene 2

The house slides halfway off revealing a restaurant. Libby and Paul are seated at a table with menus. He's quite tense.

LIBBY. I ask you for advice and you ridicule me?!

PAUL. I did *not* ridicule you!

LIBBY. You called me "risible." You used the word risible. Thus you were able to make me feel small AND show off your fancy vocabulary at the same time. Well, no one is impressed.

PAUL. I just don't see the problem.

LIBBY. I explained it. I laid it out very clearly. I have this client —

PAUL. *(Correcting her.)* John.

LIBBY. Don't use the vernacular. It makes me feel cheap. I have this *client*, Gerald, perfectly nice man, used to see him Tuesdays and he offered me a job. Second editorial assistant, *catalogue*. Well do you know what that pays?

PAUL. I have no idea.

LIBBY. It doesn't pay enough for cat food.

PAUL. You don't have a cat.

LIBBY. Luckily, or she'd starve to death. The point is, I look at this job as supplemental income. Clearly, it can't be my main source of income. I mean clearly — I don't know what the other assistants are doing, dealing drugs or something, I have no idea. So I have my regular clients and my new nine to five, which I'm looking at, strictly, as a doorway. You know, something that could lead to something that could lead to something. But I think I have to quit. I mean, I don't think I can stay there.

PAUL. *(Annoyed.)* Then quit.

LIBBY. Do you think I should?

PAUL. I have no idea. *(Andrew, crosses behind them, unnoticed. He is the waiter.)*

LIBBY. But you see my point? It's one thing to sleep with Gerald, who by the way is the hairiest human being I've ever laid eyes on — the man is one third simian — it's one thing to fuck him when I'm getting paid to fuck him. But if I'm the second editorial assistant, catalogue, and I fuck him, it's sexual harassment!

PAUL. *(Angry.)* Then quit! Just quit!

LIBBY. Well ... you're in a mood.

PAUL. You horn your way in on this lunch and then bombard me with your problems, which, I'm sorry, I'm sticking to my guns, are simply risible — I mean fuck him, don't fuck him

49

what's the difference? He pays you to fuck him, fuck him! —
Did it ever occur to you that I might have problems? I might
have something on my mind?

LIBBY.   No. Frankly, it didn't. I'm sorry I'm so self-absorbed.
I am, really. I'll try to be interested in other people — at least
in you. You have problems? You never have problems.

PAUL.   Of course I have problems!

LIBBY.   You never share them. You're very withholding. What
kind of problems? What's the matter?

PAUL.   Dolph wants to move in.

LIBBY.   Dolph?

PAUL.   The man I've been seeing.

LIBBY.   *(Thinking.)* You never mentioned a Dolph. I'd remember a Dolph.

PAUL.   I told you. You don't listen!

LIBBY.   What?

PAUL.   Skip it.

LIBBY.   His name is Dolph?

PAUL.   He's Swedish.

LIBBY.   Let's hope.

PAUL.   I don't want to talk about it.

LIBBY.   So do you think I should quit?

PAUL.   We've been dating for three weeks, a record, and I'm
very fond of him.

LIBBY.   Does he speak English?

PAUL.   Yes!

LIBBY.   Good.

PAUL.   A little. Broken English. He's very sweet. He's very attractive. The sex is fantastic!

LIBBY.   Have you seen a waiter?

PAUL.   Are you listening!?

LIBBY.   Yes. I'm sorry. He's sweet. How?

PAUL.   He's cute. He makes me things.

LIBBY.   What kind of things?

PAUL.   Cookies. Baked goods. He's a baker.

LIBBY.   He sounds like a catch. Move in with him. Dolph the
baker. I hope you'll be very happy.

PAUL.   I don't love him.

LIBBY. And you *won't* move in with him. I know you. The fact that it's been three weeks is the surprising part. You go through men much faster than I do. I mean I still have my very first client, Jack — he gave me this watch. Like it? Anniversary gift — I still have Jack and you've been through God knows how many men!

PAUL. Not that many.

LIBBY. Shall I name them?

PAUL. It's not that many.

LIBBY. There was Billy, and Charles, and Donald, *two* Davids and Derrick, and Dell —

PAUL. What's your point!?

LIBBY. I think I've made my point.

PAUL. Well, Dolph wants an answer — is there a waiter? Is this a cafeteria?

LIBBY. And what do you mean I horn my way in?

PAUL. I told you I was having lunch with Taylor and you begged me to come along —

LIBBY. I wouldn't've had to beg if you'd've invited me.

PAUL. I haven't seen Taylor in months. I'm worried about him. I wanted to see him and you know you make him uncomfortable!

LIBBY. What a terrible thing to say!

PAUL. Facts are facts.

LIBBY. I don't make him uncomfortable. I don't make anyone uncomfortable!

PAUL. Fine.

LIBBY. I make him uncomfortable?

PAUL. Yes.

LIBBY. He told you that?

PAUL. Sort of.

LIBBY. What does that mean?

PAUL. He didn't have to.

LIBBY. You just assumed —

PAUL. He intimated.

LIBBY. When?

PAUL. I don't remember.

LIBBY. He never said *anything* — did he?

PAUL. He implied it.

LIBBY. Why would I make him uncomfortable?

PAUL. Because you love him.

LIBBY. So?

PAUL. Because you love him — you're *in love* with him, obsessively, and you're very obvious about it.

LIBBY. And that makes him uncomfortable? Well, I refuse to participate in that kind hyper-sensitivity. *(Andrew approaches them, not looking up.)*

ANDREW. Sorry to keep you waiting. Can I tell you about our specials?

LIBBY. Andrew!

ANDREW. Libby?! Paul!

LIBBY. What are you doing here?!

ANDREW. Well, waiting tables, obviously.

LIBBY. How've you been?

ANDREW. I've been OK. I've been very well. Although, I got fired from Bloomingdales. I had a fit one day and broke all the crystal. Where are you living now?

PAUL. I don't think I want to tell you.

LIBBY. What kind of fit?

ANDREW. Epileptic. I had a seizure.

LIBBY. And they fired you? I bet you could sue.

ANDREW. Oh, it wasn't real. I faked it. I was angry at my manager, who said I could move in with him. Then he reneged, so I faked a seizure and destroyed the inventory.

PAUL. *(Weary.)* What are the specials?

LIBBY. Where are you living? Are you still at Paul's old place? *(Paul is distracted by something.)*

ANDREW. Oh no. I stayed there for a while. But then the people who moved in after you, a married couple, Martin and Jeanette Copeland — they bickered ALL the time and got on my nerves. So I left. Remember that name Martin and Jeanette Copeland. Avoid them. That's when I was supposed to move in with Larry, my manager. Larry ... I never knew his last name. But he decided he needed his privacy. God knows why. I mean his apartment is gigantic. Much bigger than yours. It's decorated very well and he has a dish. I mean a satellite dish. We

52

could have lived together the rest of our lives and never laid eyes on one another. I think his mother's South American or something. So, anyway, I went to this bar on Twenty-second street, and met Sven —

LIBBY. Sven?

ANDREW. He's Swedish —

LIBBY. What's going on?

ANDREW. He bought me a rum and coke — I'm drinking rum and coke these days — and we hit it off right away. I went back to his place, which is not nearly as big as Larry's, but about the same size as yours — and I've been with Sven for two months now. We're very happy.

PAUL. *(Leaning in.)* Do you think that man's attractive?

LIBBY. Who?

PAUL. That man there. In the gray coat. Do you think he's attractive? *(They all stare.)*

ANDREW. *I* do!

PAUL. He's flirting with me.

ANDREW. He comes in here all the time. I've always had a big crush on him.

LIBBY. He looks familiar.

PAUL. If he goes to the bathroom, I'm going to follow.

ANDREW. That works.

LIBBY. I know his face. I know I know his face.

ANDREW. I followed him to the bathroom once and we had sex three times —

LIBBY. I wish I could — It's Jack!

ANDREW. He told me his name was Ron.

PAUL. He's looking! *(They abruptly look away.)*

LIBBY. I don't mean his name is Jack. That's Jack's son!

ANDREW. Who's Jack?

LIBBY. A client.

ANDREW. You have a job?!

PAUL. A John.

ANDREW. Oh.

LIBBY. But yes, I have a job, thank you, second editorial assistant, catalogue. That's him. I've looked at that picture hundreds of times. I used to think it came with the frame. He's *very* attractive.

PAUL. I should send him a drink.

LIBBY. What about Dolph?

ANDREW. *(Correcting her.)* Sven.

PAUL. Who?

ANDREW. *(Correcting her.)* What about him?

LIBBY. *(To Paul.)* Don't you think —

PAUL. It's just a drink. It doesn't mean anything. And that relationship is —

LIBBY. *(Looking back.)* That man has watched his father and me have sex every Thursday for six months. In every imaginable position. I feel like I know him. I should go over. Don't you think I should?

PAUL. What?!

LIBBY. I should say hello.

PAUL. "Hello, I get paid to fuck your father?"

LIBBY. Well —

PAUL. Something like that?

ANDREW. He's in no position to judge anyone. Trust me.

LIBBY. Oh really?

ANDREW. I could tell you stories!

PAUL. What do you mean?

ANDREW. Oh, I have an order up. I'll be back. *(Andrew rushes off.)*

PAUL. Did we order?

LIBBY. No. *(Taylor enters, looking weary, disheveled. Paul stands.)*

PAUL. Taylor! *(The men embrace.)*

TAYLOR. I'm sorry I'm late.

PAUL. Libby came. I hope that's all right.

TAYLOR. What? Oh yes. Fine. Probably good. *(They sit.)*

LIBBY. Probably?

TAYLOR. Well —

LIBBY. I haven't seen you in months.

PAUL. Neither have I.

TAYLOR. I haven't gone out.

PAUL. Are you all right?

TAYLOR. What do you mean?

PAUL. I had to call twenty times before you'd pick up —

54

LIBBY. I need a drink.

PAUL. You don't call *me* and, the fact of the matter is, you've been through alot. I mean —

TAYLOR. You look well.

PAUL and LIBBY. Thank you.

LIBBY. He meant me.

PAUL. Where's Andrew?

TAYLOR. Who's Andrew?

PAUL. The waiter.

LIBBY. Paul slept with him.

TAYLOR. Just now?

PAUL. Ages ago. You remember, he's the one who wouldn't leave.

TAYLOR. Vaguely.

LIBBY. How've you been? Have you been well?

PAUL. Don't bombard him with questions.

LIBBY. *(To Taylor.)* He's in a bad mood.

PAUL. I'm not in a bad mood.

LIBBY. Fine.

PAUL. *(To Taylor.)* How *have* you been? The two of you. Is Cynthia all right? *(Taylor lights a cigarette.)*

TAYLOR. *(Flat, after a beat.)* Cynthia left.

PAUL. What?

TAYLOR. She left.

PAUL. What do you mean?!

TAYLOR. I came home. I came home from work one day. I came home and she was gone. That's what I mean. I don't know why or where she went ... I mean she's gone. She left. *(Taylor is near tears. There is a pause.)*

LIBBY. *(Gently.)* Well, maybe it's for the best —

TAYLOR. What?

LIBBY. I just mean —

PAUL. What do you mean you don't know?

TAYLOR. I came home and she was gone. Her things were gone.

PAUL. Oh my God.

TAYLOR. All of her dresses. All of her clothes.

PAUL. Where is she?

TAYLOR.   I don't know.

PAUL.   Oh my God.

TAYLOR.   *(To Libby.)* Have you heard from her?

LIBBY.   No.

TAYLOR.   She hasn't called?

LIBBY.   No.

PAUL.   When was this?

TAYLOR.   A month, five weeks.

LIBBY.   God I'm thirsty.

PAUL.   She just left?

TAYLOR.   *(To Libby.)* I called your parents. They had a message, but just that she was fine.

PAUL.   One day? No warning?

TAYLOR.   *(To Libby.)* No number.

PAUL.   Was there a note?

TAYLOR.   Yes.

PAUL.   What did it say?

LIBBY.   Do you want to talk about it?

PAUL.   What did it say?

TAYLOR.   It didn't say anything.

PAUL.   It must've said something.

LIBBY.   *(Quietly.)* I hate her.

PAUL.   Libby.

LIBBY.   I do.

TAYLOR.   *(To Paul.)* It didn't.

PAUL.   Well was it a blank piece of paper? Or was it a note?

TAYLOR.   It said good-bye. All right? It said good-bye.

PAUL.   One word?

TAYLOR.   Yes. One word.

PAUL.   Well. We'll just have to wait.

TAYLOR.   We?

PAUL.   You.

TAYLOR.   We don't have to talk about this. I just wanted to know if you'd heard anything. If she'd called you.

LIBBY.   We can talk about it.

TAYLOR.   I don't want to, frankly.

LIBBY.   You're sure?

PAUL.   Are you all right?

TAYLOR. I'm fine.

PAUL. By yourself. Out there. All alone?

TAYLOR. It's fine.

PAUL. I could visit. I could come and visit.

TAYLOR. *(Snapping.)* LET'S TALK ABOUT SOMETHING ELSE —

PAUL. I'm sorry.

TAYLOR. ALL RIGHT?

PAUL. I'm just ... if you need to talk — *(Taylor puts out his cigarette.)*

TAYLOR. How's — Carl?

PAUL. Who?

TAYLOR. I can't remember his name.

LIBBY. Sven.

PAUL. *(Correcting her.)* Dolph.

TAYLOR. That's it.

PAUL. He's fine.

TAYLOR. Good.

PAUL. I think that's ending. I think that's run it's course. *(Andrew approaches.)*

ANDREW. I'm back. I'm sorry about that. We're under-staffed today. Should I tell you about the specials, or do you want to order drinks?

LIBBY. A glass of white wine.

PAUL. Diet coke.

TAYLOR. Jack Daniels. *(Andrew nods and exits. Libby and Paul notice that he's ordered alcohol.)*

LIBBY. Taylor?

TAYLOR. What?

LIBBY. *(After a long beat.)* Nothing. *(The three of them sit silently as the light fades out.)*

Scene 3

The house slides off the rest of the way revealing an apartment, or the suggestion of one. Cynthia is finishing getting dressed to go out. After a moment, Libby enters, dressed as she

57

was in the last scene, having come from lunch. Cynthia stops
what she's doing.

CYNTHIA.   Did you see him.
LIBBY.   Yes.
CYNTHIA.   Did you tell him?
LIBBY.   No.
CYNTHIA.   Thank you. *(Relieved, Cynthia seems to become her old self.)*
LIBBY.   He drank.
CYNTHIA.   Oh?
LIBBY.   Where are you going?
CYNTHIA.   Out.
LIBBY.   Oh?
CYNTHIA.   Dr. Allen.
LIBBY.   Oh.
CYNTHIA.   He is the sweetest man! *(Cynthia leaves. Libby is left alone. Fade out.)*

Scene 4

A light comes up on Andrew, who addresses the audience.

ANDREW.   The thing about Sven ... is his beauty. And I don't mean that "inner beauty" people talk about, although, I suppose he's got beauty inside of him. I never really thought about it. Frankly I think "inner beauty" is a little too much to hope for. "Nice" is the best we can expect to find. And he is nice. But more than that he's beautiful. And although, I'm often attracted to men whose beauty is idiosyncratic at best — I mean I've often found myself defending my taste, because, frankly, I find weak chins sexy and I'd much rather go to bed with someone who has a few pounds to lose than someone who looks like an advertisement for an exercise machine — Sven is beautiful in an *absolutely objective* manner. Everyone thinks so. Men, women, children, dogs. Blind people know he's beautiful! He looks like a big, fucking, Nordic God. And, as I said, he's nice.

So I don't mind that he only gets basic cable. I don't mind because, oddly, and this is not false modesty, Sven, against *all logic*, thinks I'm beautiful too. You see, I know I don't belong in the circus, but I also know I don't belong on magazine covers. I'm fine. And the fact that this Scandinavian Adonis thinks I'm beautiful seems more than a coincidence, it seems like fate. — He has flaws, mind you. He can be moody, and childish and sometimes I think he steals. But he has this wonderful pseudo-British accent, having been taught English overseas, that makes his most idiotic babble sound like the musings of a Nobel Prize winner. — Oh, I'll get him. He didn't want to come out, he's shy, which is odd considering his looks, but I'll make him and you can meet him for yourself. *(As Andrew rushes off. A light comes up on Taylor who addresses the audience.)*

TAYLOR. At the meetings, when I went to meetings, I remember hearing that phrase over and over again. You know, the one about being powerless. They all adopt it and adapt it to their needs. Powerless over drugs, powerless over alcohol, over food, over lust. But I believe I had found a higher power, my higher power. I found it one night, one summer night, when I had just started trying save myself. I'd been out with Libby, who never really showed much interest in saving herself, we'd been to a movie and I drove her home, to her parents house. She was going to stay there for the weekend. I pulled up, and there, sitting on the lawn was her sister, Cynthia.... That seems like years ago. And then so many things happened. I can't even remember them all. *(Taylor's light goes out and light comes up on Libby, who addresses the audience. As she speaks the light around her, in her apartment comes up slowly.)*

LIBBY. For six weeks, after that lunch, I kept my secret: that Cynthia was living with me. She knocked on my door one day, unannounced, with her luggage and dissolved before my eyes. What was I supposed to do? But after that day, seeing Taylor, seeing him in pain, in trouble, seeing him drinking ... well I called him all the time. I called every day. At different times. But it was always the machine and Cynthia's voice, cheerful, pleasant, polite, between us. I called his office but he was never there. He didn't go in much, or at all, and no one there knew why exactly, except that he was sick. And every night I laid awake, thinking about him, wishing there was something I could do. And with my *clients* there were times when my mind would wonder away from my work. I'd be under some middle-aged man imitating feelings and I would start to think about Taylor. And I would just … cry. Sometimes quietly, sometimes great heaving sobs. But these clients, who are nice men, for the most part, seldom even noticed. Except Jack, my first client, who gave me this watch. He noticed. He stopped — what he was doing — and asked me what was wrong. I was really weeping at this point. And I told him, looking at him, just unable to hurt him, that it was nothing. That it was just that, I wished, somehow I could afford to be with him for free. That I cared about him, but that I would never know how he really felt about me because of our "arrangement." He was very touched and looked like he might cry too. *(Smiling, touched by this.)* And then, he did a really remarkable thing. He kissed my eyes, in the dark, and asked me, he said, "Do you think … would you like … would you like … to get married?"… It was the saddest question I have ever heard. And after a long time I said, "I don't know." And then he resumed, he returned to the task at hand. But it was different. It was gentler than it had been and he didn't flinch when a car drove by and the light from the headlights came through the window. He didn't panic at the idea that I might see him. Of course I didn't see him, because I was with Taylor, feeling Taylor, holding him, touching him … helping him. Paul kept me posted. They didn't speak often, but he wasn't doing well. And finally, I couldn't stand it any longer. *(Cynthia enters, cheerful. They start the scene with any hostility well concealed.)*

CYNTHIA.   Dr. Allen could *not* be nicer!

LIBBY.   *(Getting a drink.)* I don't understand what you're doing.

CYNTHIA.   What do you mean?

LIBBY.   Are you "dating" this person?

CYNTHIA.   *(Pleasant.)* You've been drinking again, haven't you?

LIBBY.   I'm drinking *now*.

CYNTHIA.   You drink too much and then you say ugly things.

You drink too much because you're afraid of people — *and* being alone. Ending up alone. That's why you do what you do. Sex with all those faceless strangers. Those needy, pathetic —

LIBBY.   *(Abruptly.)* I don't think you should stay here. I'm sorry, but I think — I don't think you should.

CYNTHIA.   Fine. I'll look for something as soon as I get back.

LIBBY.   Get back?

CYNTHIA.   Dr. Allen's invited me to Italy.

LIBBY.   You're going to Italy?

CYNTHIA.   I can't imagine that it's any of your business.

LIBBY.   What about Taylor?

CYNTHIA.   It's only two weeks.

LIBBY.   I have to tell him.

CYNTHIA.   No.

LIBBY.   That your here. That you're going away, but you're here.

CYNTHIA.   *(Deadly.)* I will *never* forgive you. *(A light comes up on Paul.)*

PAUL.   She's been there all this time!?

LIBBY.   Yes.

PAUL.   You kept this from me!? You kept it from Taylor!!?

LIBBY.   *(To Paul.)* I'm sorry.

CYNTHIA.   I will never forgive you. *(Cynthia exits.)*

PAUL.   *(Disbelief.)* How could you?!

LIBBY.   She's my sister.

PAUL.   I thought you cared about him!?

LIBBY.   I'm sorry!

PAUL.   You sat at that lunch —

LIBBY.   I'M SORRY!

PAUL.   You sat there and lied!?

LIBBY.   She won't see him.

PAUL.   She has to.

LIBBY.   If she knows he's coming, she'll leave.

PAUL.   Don't tell her.

LIBBY.   She'll hide. She'll lock the door. The bedroom door.

PAUL.   This is insane!

LIBBY.   She refuses to see him. She says she can't. She's going away.

PAUL.   When!?

LIBBY.   I'm not sure. To Italy. With her doctor.

PAUL.   Do you expect *me* not to tell him?!

LIBBY.   Maybe you shouldn't. What's the point if it's over. Maybe a clean break is better.

PAUL.   Taylor will die! *(Paul's light goes out leaving Libby alone. After a moment, Libby's light goes out. Andrew rushes into a pool of light.)*

ANDREW.   Well, he won't come out. And now we have had our first fight.

Scene 5

The light comes up slowly on Taylor's house, late at night. Hopefully this is the same piece as the exterior, flipped. Paul is seated, alone at first. The room is dark and shadowy. After a moment, Taylor enters, wearing a tee-shirt, pajama bottoms and a bathrobe. He looks tired, worn-out, and carries a glass of whisky and a plate of cookies. During the scene Taylor occasionally shakes a tiny bit, exhibits a tiny tremor.

TAYLOR.   I'm afraid all I have is some cookies. *(He hands the plate to Paul, who takes one and sets it down. Taylor does not sit. They seem to talk around things.)*

PAUL.   That's all right.

TAYLOR.   I'm sorry.

PAUL.   I love cookies.

TAYLOR.   Your sure you don't want a drink?

PAUL.   I'm sure.

TAYLOR.   I think I'll have one. *(He sips his drink.)*

PAUL.   I hope you don't mind my coming by.

TAYLOR.   Not at all.

PAUL.   I tried to call but I got the machine.

TAYLOR.   Oh, yes. I have it turned down, and the phone, so I don't hear the ring. I'm glad you came. It's nice to see you.

PAUL.   But your not dressed. Maybe I should —

TAYLOR.   It *is* one-thirty. I was ...

PAUL. Were you in bed?

TAYLOR. No, no. It's good to see you. You look well. How've you been? Have you been well?

PAUL. Fine. I suppose. Worried about you.

TAYLOR. Oh?

PAUL. I spoke to Libby, today.

TAYLOR. How is she doing? Is she still...?

PAUL. She is.

TAYLOR. Isn't that amazing. I mean, she's not what you think. You know, she's not the cliché at all. Is she?

PAUL. I suppose not. The terrible thing is she's gotten used to it now. You know, living that way. It doesn't bother her any more. I try not to judge. In the abstract I have no problem. But it's Libby.

TAYLOR. You get used to things. Things become your life.

PAUL. How are you?

TAYLOR. I'm all right.

PAUL. Are you? Are you doing better?

TAYLOR. *(Merely interested.)* I seem to shake sometimes. I've developed this shake, this tremor. It comes and goes.

PAUL. You should see a doctor.

TAYLOR. He'd just tell me not to drink.

PAUL. You shouldn't then.

TAYLOR. But I prefer it. I prefer being slightly out of touch. You know?

PAUL. You were doing so well.

TAYLOR. That was before. I hope you're not going to lecture me. I hope you didn't come all this way to "talk" to me. I mean I appreciate the good intentions. But please don't. I know you care about me. I care about you. My God, we've known each other since we were six years old. But, I have to tell you I won't be "talked to." Do you understand?

PAUL. Yes.

TAYLOR. Because I'm doing what I want.

PAUL. I just wish there was something ...

TAYLOR. *(Flat, not sad.)* You see the thing is, I know that I'm killing myself. I paid attention at those meetings. I took everything in. But I find, and please don't over-react, because it's just the way it is, I find that I don't really *want* to live any more.

PAUL.   Taylor.

TAYLOR.   I sound stupid probably. But there you are. I wouldn't worry too much. I don't have a lot of courage. I was never the type to really do things for myself. Went to work for my father. Dried out for Cynthia. So I wouldn't worry. The other day I took out a gun. My father had guns. Did you know that? A man who made toys for a living collected guns. I went up, into the attic and dug one out. A little gun, a pistol. And I held it and I looked at it. It was sort amazing to me. I mean this small piece of metal that I held in my hand had so much power.... But then I put it away ... *(He starts to cry, just a bit.)* She might come back. People come back. I wish she would call.

PAUL.   You need some help, Taylor.

TAYLOR.   *(Composing himself.)* Oh, I know. I know I do. But I don't want any help. I'm fine.

PAUL.   You can't say you don't want to live in one breath and tell me you're fine in the next.

TAYLOR.   I just don't want to think about things! I know this will pass. Everything does, one way or another. But I don't want to think right now. Because I don't understand. It's not fair. Something terrible happened. To us. Both of us. And I failed.

PAUL.   No one failed.

TAYLOR.   She helped me so much, but when something happened to *us* I didn't know what to. I tried. I did. I tried to figure it out. Day by day. Minute by minute, those first weeks. I tried to know what she needed, what she wanted. And the harder I tried, the angrier she got. Until she couldn't take it anymore. And she went away.

PAUL.   She's doing what she needs to. I suppose.

TAYLOR.   I suppose.

PAUL.   But you can't give up on everything.

TAYLOR.   Of course I can. Why can't I?

PAUL.   Because there are people who care about you.

TAYLOR.   I understand that.

PAUL.   You're much stronger than you think.

TAYLOR.   But I'm not as strong as you think. People look at me, I know this, people look at me and think I'm attractive.

People give me things. They think I am my face. But I'm not. I look in the mirror and I know I'm not.

PAUL. You're just feeling sorry for yourself.

TAYLOR. I don't feel sorry. I feel angry. Well, not angry really.... You're probably right.

PAUL. I can stay out here. With you, if you want. For a little while.

TAYLOR. Don't you have work?

PAUL. It doesn't matter.

TAYLOR. You have a life.

PAUL. I'll stay.

TAYLOR. No. Not now. It wouldn't make any difference. It was Cynthia. And now she's gone and I find I don't want to live anymore, which even as I repeat it, embarrasses me.... You're sure you don't want a drink? *(There is a pause, during which Paul decides to tell him.)*

PAUL. I spoke to Libby today.

TAYLOR. You said that.

PAUL. Cynthia's with her.

TAYLOR. *(Dropping his glass.)* Take me.

PAUL. She won't see you.

TAYLOR. Take me!

PAUL. She doesn't want to see you.

TAYLOR. I'm going —

PAUL. Wait. Maybe you should wait.

TAYLOR. Why? Why!? For what?

PAUL. She's hiding. If she's hiding, if she doesn't want to see you, maybe you should wait. Not force yourself. Give her some time.

TAYLOR. What do you mean hiding!?

PAUL. Libby says she refuses to see you.

TAYLOR. She's my wife!

PAUL. She's going away.

TAYLOR. Did you talk to her!?

PAUL. No.

TAYLOR. I want to see her!

PAUL. Maybe you should wait until she gets back. You can't go forcing her. You can't force things. Give her some time.

TAYLOR. How much time!?

PAUL. I don't know.

TAYLOR. A day? Two days? A week? A year?

PAUL. She's going away for two weeks. Why don't you wait and see —

TAYLOR. I can't.

PAUL. She's running away. Obviously.

TAYLOR. From me?

PAUL. If you go there. Now. Like this —

TAYLOR. I need her.

PAUL. I know that.

TAYLOR. Will you talk to her?

PAUL. Yes.

TAYLOR. Ask her to see me. Ask her not to go.

PAUL. I will, tomorrow.

TAYLOR. She could be gone!

PAUL. She won't be.

TAYLOR. Tell her I love her.

PAUL. I will.

TAYLOR. Tell her I know that I fucked up. I know that things — tell her to come home.

PAUL. I will.

TAYLOR. Do you think she'll come?

PAUL. I don't know.

TAYLOR. She will. She will.

PAUL. I'll go tomorrow.

TAYLOR. Bring her back. Here, with you.

PAUL. I'll try.

TAYLOR. Thank you.

PAUL. I'll do my best. *(Paul puts his coat on.)*

TAYLOR. Will you be all right? Getting back?

PAUL. I'll be fine.

TAYLOR. How long has she been at Libby's?

PAUL. The whole time.

TAYLOR. Oh?

PAUL. Since she left.

TAYLOR. All these weeks, months?

PAUL. Yes.

TAYLOR. Why wouldn't Libby tell me?

PAUL. I don't know.

TAYLOR. Just tell me where she was. That she was all right?

PAUL. Maybe Libby didn't *want* to help you.

TAYLOR. Oh. (*Paul think for a moment. It occurs to him that what he is about to say is true of himself as well.*)

PAUL. Maybe Libby doesn't want to see you back together.

TAYLOR. Yes, of course.

PAUL. I'll talk to Cynthia.

TAYLOR. I love you. (*The men embrace as the light fades out.*)

Scene 6

A pool of light comes up on Andrew, who addresses the audience.

ANDREW. We were in bed, Sven and I — well actually Sven was in bed and I was on the floor. I was giving him a foot massage with hand cream. — He loves that. He gets a delirious, infantile grin on his face and actually makes a purring sound — And the phone rang. He started talking Swedish, very fast and very agitated and I knew that something was wrong. And the color, what color there is, which is minimal given he's Scandinavian, drained from his face. Eventually, he hung up. I let him sit for minute, figuring he'd tell me what it was when he was ready. He did. It was his mother, in Stockholm. Sven's mother is 84, he has older siblings, and she'd had a stroke. I thought, well, naturally, he's upset. I will *try* to comfort him. I will be useful to him. I assumed he was upset because his mother was clinging to life by her Swedish fingernails. But as we packed his things, for his trip home, he told me no. He wasn't upset about that. He *loathed* his mother and she'd lived a very productive life, producing *and alienating* seven children is an achievement by anyone's standards. No. He was upset that he'd have to leave me. Even for a week. Even for a day. I want to be gracious and just accept his love, but I can't help wondering if Sven's complete devotion to me isn't proof that beauty and brains really are mutually exclusive.... I love him. (*Andrew's light goes out.*)

67

Scene 7

Libby's apartment, evening. She is seated. Paul is pacing. On the other side of the stage, the back of the house and the lawn have reappeared.

PAUL. Where could she be?

LIBBY. I don't know. She doesn't tell me where she goes.

PAUL. What time is it?

LIBBY. Seven — She doesn't tell me what she does.

PAUL. Did you tell her I was coming?

LIBBY. We hardly speak at all. Just the basics. "So and so called." "Be quiet." And "pass the salt." That's it. To say we had a chilly rapport would be generous.

PAUL. He didn't have any food. Some cookies. That was it. Cookies.

LIBBY. Please don't talk about it.

PAUL. Why? It's not *your* fault. *(Cynthia enters, bright, in her coat.)*

CYNTHIA. Paul!

LIBBY. It's home. *(Cynthia kisses Paul on the cheek.)*

CYNTHIA. What a surprise!

LIBBY. Where have you been?

CYNTHIA. Out. I had some errands to run.

PAUL. Hello Cynthia.

CYNTHIA. Look at you! I haven't seen you in forever! Did Libby offer you drink? Did you offer him a drink?

LIBBY. *(Sarcastic.)* No. I drank all the liquor and offered him oyster crackers.

CYNTHIA. *(To Libby.)* You're not working tonight?

LIBBY. The fleet left town.

CYNTHIA. I asked a simple question.

LIBBY. Sorry.

CYNTHIA. How've you been Paul?

PAUL. Fine.

CYNTHIA. Have you been here long?

PAUL. Yes.

CYNTHIA. Oh. I'm sorry. Were you waiting for me? I had no idea. I'd've come home — I mean here — sooner. I had all kinds of things I had to get accomplished. Details. I'm going away. No doubt Libby told you that. She loves talking about me. For some reason I fascinate her. — What have you been up to?

PAUL. Please don't be social.

CYNTHIA. What?

PAUL. Don't be charming. Please.

CYNTHIA. Well…. I think I'll go to my room. I have a lot of packing to do, and I'm sure the two of you want your privacy — to do whatever it is you do.

PAUL. I need to talk to you.

CYNTHIA. I'm not feeling very well. I was running around all day —

PAUL. I've been to see Taylor.

CYNTHIA. And I forgot to eat.

PAUL. He's not well.

CYNTHIA. Oh?

PAUL. Libby tells me you won't see him.

CYNTHIA. Thank you, Libby.

LIBBY. Don't mention it.

PAUL. I'm concerned.

CYNTHIA. You're a good friend.

PAUL. Please see him.

CYNTHIA. *(After a beat.)* No.

PAUL. Please.

CYNTHIA. Is he here? Did you bring him? Is he part of this?

PAUL. No. Come back with me.

CYNTHIA. I can't.

PAUL. Why not?

CYNTHIA. I'm sorry, Paul, but I don't think I owe you an explanation. I've made a decision. I stick to my decisions. Always have. Ask Libby. I've decided this and it's something, it's *one thing* I can control. Now, I appreciate that you care for Taylor, that you hardly know me, but that he's important to you. You've done what you wanted, come here, on his behalf and asked me. I've said no. You're finished. You've done your best.

PAUL.   I don't understand. Is it — Is it over? I mean —
CYNTHIA.   *(Slightly hostile.)* What is your place in this? What exactly, is your role?
PAUL.   I care about my friend.
CYNTHIA.   Then don't you think it's better — I mean you tell me he's not doing well — don't you think it's better, that he will *get better*, faster, sooner, if he faces things, facts?
PAUL.   You don't understand —
LIBBY.   Don't you think —
CYNTHIA.   *(Snapping.)* I've said what I think.
PAUL.   He's drinking.
CYNTHIA.   People drink.
PAUL.   He's drinking too much. Maybe drugs. I don't know.
CYNTHIA.   He did all of that before! And he survived.
PAUL.   He hasn't worked!
CYNTHIA.   He never liked work. He never liked it there!
PAUL.   Listen to me! There was no food! There was nothing in his house. He doesn't sleep or eat or answer the phone. He doesn't go out! He shakes, like — I don't know — an old man — Listen to me!
CYNTHIA.   NO!
PAUL.   Cynthia.
CYNTHIA.   You come into my home —
LIBBY.   *My* home.
CYNTHIA.   You come *here* and expect me to do something!
PAUL.   I do! Yes. He's your husband!
CYNTHIA.   I'm not capable! I can't do what you want! It's not fair of you to ask. Now please leave!
PAUL.   He says he doesn't want to live anymore.
CYNTHIA.   What is that supposed to mean!? *(Across the stage Taylor appears. He sits in the doorway, looking up at the sky.)*
PAUL.   He has a gun — his father's gun.
CYNTHIA.   I'm not responsible! I don't accept responsibility!
PAUL.   I'm worried —
LIBBY.   *(Entreating.)* Cynthia.
PAUL.   What if he does something?
CYNTHIA.   Why would he!?
PAUL.   You didn't see him!

CYNTHIA.   I don't have to! People don't kill themselves over
— what? Over nothing! I've never heard of anything so absurd!
A failed romance? Broken marriage? Happens everyday!
PAUL.   And people —
CYNTHIA.   He has to move on!! These things happen! Every-
one's had something, some tragedy, happen to them! And this
adolescent idea that Taylor would do something, hurt himself
— it's just absurd! I won't participate in this *hysteria!*
PAUL.   Listen to me!
CYNTHIA.   *(Attacking now.)* You tell me he's sick! You tell me
he's drinking! Doesn't want to live —
PAUL.   I'm not an alarmist —
LIBBY.   Just see him!
PAUL.   I'm scared!
CYNTHIA.   What am I supposed to do!?
PAUL.   Come back with me!
CYNTHIA.   Why?!
PAUL.   He needs you!
LIBBY.   You owe him that —
CYNTHIA.   So he can beg me!? He does!
PAUL.   Say good-bye!
CYNTHIA.   It won't be good-bye!
LIBBY.   Just see him!
PAUL.   Please!
LIBBY.   Cynthia.
PAUL.   Talk to him.
LIBBY.   See him! *(Cynthia explodes in a way we have never seen, a
mixture of intense rage and fear at once.)*
CYNTHIA.   NO!! NO!! STOP!! STOP THIS!! YOU HAVE NO
RIGHT! YOU HAVE NO RIGHT TO ASK ME THIS! WHAT
HAPPENED, WHAT HAS HAPPENED HAPPENED TO ME!!
ME!! MY BODY!! MY CHILD!! MY SON!! I NEVER HELD MY
SON! I NEVER SAW HIM!! MY CHILD DIED!! HIS NAME
WAS JEFFREY!! HIS NAME WAS JEFFREY AND HE DIED!
STRANGLED! SUFFOCATED IN *MY BODY!* STRANGLED *BY
MY BODY!!* I SAW A BOX! A TINY BOX!! AND IT WAS MY
CHILD, JEFFREY WHO STRANGLED IN *MY BODY!!* AND
YOU WANT ME TO HELP *YOUR FRIEND!!* I CAN NOT!! *I'VE*

DONE TOO MUCH TO HIM ALREADY!! I WON'T SEE HIM!! AND YOU HAVE NO RIGHT TO ASK ME! YOU HAVE NO RIGHT! *(Cynthia collapses into herself in tears. There is a long pause, but neither Libby nor Paul go to her. They watch, stunned, guilty and immobile.)* ... I don't want ... to see Taylor ... Jeffrey would have been ... a beautiful child. I know that.

PAUL.   I'm sorry.

CYNTHIA.   *(After a pause.)* The doctor said ... there was no air.

LIBBY.   *(Gently.)* It was Taylor's child too. *(Paul looks at Libby, concerned.)*

CYNTHIA.   He would have been beautiful.

LIBBY.   I know. *(Cynthia looks at Libby for a long moment, then drops her head.)*

CYNTHIA.   Tell Taylor to come in the morning. Before I leave. *To say good-bye. (Paul nods and gets his coat. Cynthia smiles a bit.)*

PAUL.   Good-bye. *(Libby walks him to the door and kisses him on the cheek.)*

LIBBY.   Give him my love. *(Paul nods and exits. There is a pause.)* I'm sorry.

CYNTHIA.   *(Flat, composed.)* Yes. I'm sure.

LIBBY.   Things will work out. You'll see.

CYNTHIA.   I'm sure.

LIBBY.   You'll feel better.

CYNTHIA.   Hmmmm.

LIBBY.   After tomorrow.

CYNTHIA.   I'm sure.

LIBBY.   Are you hungry?

CYNTHIA.   I have to pack. *(Cynthia stands and leaves the room. Libby sits and thinks. Across the stage Paul enters, not from the house, from the wing, as if he has walked around the house, knowing where to find Taylor, who is still seated in the doorway. Taylor sees him and looks up at once.)*

TAYLOR.   Did you see her? *(There is a long pause.)*

PAUL.   I'm sorry.

TAYLOR.   She wouldn't?

PAUL.   I tried.

TAYLOR.   Thank you.

PAUL.   It could be best.

TAYLOR.   Thank you.

PAUL.   I can stay here tonight. I think I should. *(Without speaking, Taylor stands and goes into the house, shutting the door behind him, leaving Paul alone. After a moment there is a gunshot. Blackout.)*

Scene 8

A light comes up on Taylor, who addresses the audience.

TAYLOR.   I didn't die. I wasn't hurt. I didn't shoot myself. I had the gun in my hand, my father's gun and I was standing in front of the mirror. I didn't mean to shoot myself. I looked in the mirror and I pointed the gun, at him. I killed him. I meant to. I shot him. *(Taylor's light goes out as a light comes up on Andrew, who addresses the audience.)*

ANDREW.   Sven's been gone two weeks and I'm watering his plants and I can smell him on the sheets. The first week we talked every night on the phone. I put his picture in front of me so I could look at him while I listened. It's a beautiful picture. Of course it doesn't capture him in his three-dimensional perfection, but it's stunning just the same. I brought it, so I could show it to you. But I got mugged on my way here. *(The light comes up on Libby's apartment. Libby is alone, at first, as she was. Cynthia enters, composed.)*

CYNTHIA.   Well I hope I didn't forget anything. If I did, I suppose I can buy it there.

LIBBY.   You'll want to anyway.

CYNTHIA.   I have no idea what the weather's like.

LIBBY.   Neither do I.

CYNTHIA.   Cold, I assume.

LIBBY.   Can I ask you something? For myself, for my ... sanity. Can I ask you something?

CYNTHIA.   What?

LIBBY.   Did you love him? Taylor. At the beginning? *(There is a long pause.)*

CYNTHIA.   Why do you ask? You already know. *(Libby is moved by Cynthia's response. The light comes up on Taylor's house. Paul is*

73

seated in the doorway. Taylor appears behind him, his hair is wet and he's wearing a bathrobe. He sits with Paul.)

PAUL. How was your shower?

TAYLOR. It was good.

PAUL. Good.

TAYLOR. Thank you for staying.

PAUL. Can I tell you something?

TAYLOR. Can I stop you?

PAUL. I know it's hard right now, but you'll see, things will be fine. Just fine. I can't help thinking, that you're lucky.

TAYLOR. Oh?

PAUL. To feel what you've felt. That depth of feeling. It's rare. Someone loving you is important, I know, but — just to feel what you have felt. I can't help thinking that you're lucky. It can be enough. It can be enough to last forever.

TAYLOR. You think?

PAUL. I know. *(Paul and Taylor look at each other. Taylor knows that Paul is talking about himself and his feeling for Taylor. He simply smiles. Cynthia sits next to Libby.)*

LIBBY. I forgot to tell you that Jack, the man who gave me this watch, asked me to marry him.

CYNTHIA. Really?

LIBBY. I've kept him waiting and waiting. It seemed ridiculous to me at first. I just didn't want to hurt him.

CYNTHIA. What are you going to do?

LIBBY. *(Hopeful, at peace.)* I have no idea.

ANDREW. The second week he was gone he called less often, but we spoke longer. His mother, it seems, just refuses to die. The whole family has a pet name for her. It's Swedish so I can't pronounce it but it means mule. As soon as she dies Sven will come home at once. He told me he'll take his luggage to the funeral and he doesn't care what anybody thinks. It occurred to me, this morning, that these weeks, with Sven gone, that this is the very first time I have ever lived alone. I thought I would hate it. I thought the sound of my own voice would drive me insane. But you know I don't talk to myself when I'm alone. And all in all, I think it's good. I love Sven completely. But I think it's good. I'm learning, I think, not to need him. *(Paul and Taylor are as they were.)*

PAUL.   I remember when we met. It was right here. I was six years old and my family lived just over there. I saw you, from my yard. You were blonder then and it was a sunny day so your hair was very bright. I don't think I'd developed any real aesthetic yet, but I knew what drew my eye. So I crossed the yard and introduced myself.

TAYLOR.   I remember that.

PAUL.   There was a tether ball court.

TAYLOR.   And I forced you to play.

PAUL.   And of course you won.

TAYLOR.   I remember that. *(The light fades out on all of them.)*

CURTAIN

PROPERTY LIST

Cigarette (PAUL)
Bottle of champagne (LIBBY)
Cigarette (LIBBY)
Stray sock (PAUL)
Drinks (TAYLOR)
Unassembled tricycle (TAYLOR)
Cigarette (TAYLOR)
Drink (LIBBY)
Plate of cookies (TAYLOR)
Glass of whiskey (TAYLOR)

SOUND EFFECT

Gunshot

NEW PLAWS

★ **CLOSER by Patrick Marber.** Winner of the 1998 Olivier Award for Best Play and the 1999 New York Drama Critics Circle Award for Best Foreign Play. Four lives intertwine over the course of four and a half years in this densely plotted, stinging look at modern love and betrayal. "CLOSER is a sad, savvy, often funny play that casts a steely, unblinking gaze at the world of relationships and lets you come to your own conclusions … CLOSER does not merely hold your attention; it burrows into you." –*New York Magazine* "A powerful, darkly funny play about the cosmic collision between the sun of love and the comet of desire." –*Newsweek Magazine* [2M, 2W] ISBN: 0-8222-1722-8

★ **THE MOST FABULOUS STORY EVER TOLD by Paul Rudnick.** A stage manager, headset and prompt book at hand, brings the house lights to half, then dark, and cues the creation of the world. Throughout the play, she's in control of everything. In other words, she's either God, or she thinks she is. "Line by line, Mr. Rudnick may be the funniest writer for the stage in the United States today … One-liners, epigrams, withering put-downs and flashing repartee: These are the candles that Mr. Rudnick lights instead of cursing the darkness … a testament to the virtues of laughing … and in laughter, there is something like the memory of Eden." –*The NY Times* "Funny it is … consistently, rapaciously, deliriously … easily the funniest play in town." –*Variety* [4M, 5W] ISBN: 0-8222-1720-1

★ **A DOLL'S HOUSE by Henrik Ibsen, adapted by Frank McGuinness.** Winner of the 1997 Tony Award for Best Revival. "New, raw, gut-twisting and gripping. Easily the hottest drama this season." –*USA Today* "Bold, brilliant and alive." –*The Wall Street Journal* "A thunderclap of an evening that takes your breath away." –*Time Magazine* [4M, 4W, 2 boys] ISBN: 0-8222-1636-1

★ **THE HERBAL BED by Peter Whelan.** The play is based on actual events which occurred in Stratford-upon-Avon in the summer of 1613, when William Shakespeare's elder daughter was publicly accused of having a sexual liaison with a married neighbor and family friend. "In his probing new play, THE HERBAL BED … Peter Whelan muses about a sidelong event in the life of Shakespeare's family and creates a finely textured tapestry of love and lies in the early 17th-century Stratford." –*The NY Times* "It is a first rate drama with interesting moral issues of truth and expediency." –*The NY Post* [5M, 3W] ISBN: 0-8222-1675-2

★ **SNAKEBIT by David Marshall Grant.** A study of modern friendship when put to the test. "… a rather smart and absorbing evening of water-cooler theater, the intimate sort of Off-Broadway experience that has you picking apart the recognizable characters long after the curtain calls." – *The NY Times* "Off-Broadway keeps on presenting us with compelling reasons for going to the theater. The latest is SNAKEBIT, David Marshall Grant's smart new comic drama about being thirtysomething and losing one's way in life." –*The NY Daily News* [3M, 1W] ISBN: 0-8222-1724-4

★ **A QUESTION OF MERCY by David Rabe.** The Obie Award-winning playwright probes the sensitive and controversial issue of doctor-assisted suicide in the age of AIDS in this poignant drama. "There are many devastating ironies in Mr. Rabe's beautifully considered, piercingly clear-eyed work …" –*The NY Times* "With unsettling candor and disturbing insight, the play arouses pity and understanding of a troubling subject … Rabe's provocative tale is an affirmation of dignity that rings clear and true." –*Variety* [6M, 1W] ISBN: 0-8222-1643-4

★ **DIMLY PERCEIVED THREATS TO THE SYSTEM by Jon Klein.** Reality and fantasy overlap with hilarious results as this unforgettable family attempts to survive the nineties. "Here's a play whose point about fractured families goes to the heart, mind – and ears." –*The Washington Post* "… an end-of-the millennium comedy about a family on the verge of a nervous breakdown … Trenchant and hilarious …" –*The Baltimore Sun* [2M, 4W] ISBN: 0-8222-1677-9

DRAMATISTS PLAY SERVICE, INC.
440 Park Avenue South, New York, NY 10016 212-683-8960 Fax 212-213-1539
postmaster@dramatists.com www.dramatists.com

NEW PLAYS

★ **AS BEES IN HONEY DROWN by Douglas Carter Beane.** Winner of the John Gassner Playwriting Award. A hot young novelist finds the subject of his new screenplay in a New York socialite who leads him into the world of *Auntie Mame* and *Breakfast at Tiffany's*, before she takes him for a ride. "A delicious soufflé of a satire ... [an] extremely entertaining fable for an age that always chooses image over substance." *–The NY Times* "... A witty assessment of one of the most active and relentless industries in a consumer society ... the creation of 'hot' young things, which the media have learned to mass produce with efficiency and zeal." *–The NY Daily News* [3M, 3W, flexible casting] ISBN: 0-8222-1651-5

★ **STUPID KIDS by John C. Russell.** In rapid, highly stylized scenes, the story follows four high-school students as they make their way from first through eighth period and beyond, struggling with the fears, frustrations, and longings peculiar to youth. "In STUPID KIDS ... playwright John C. Russell gets the opera of adolescence to a T ... The stylized teenspeak of STUPID KIDS ... suggests that Mr. Russell may have hidden a tape recorder under a desk in study hall somewhere and then scoured the tapes for good quotations ... it is the kids' insular, ceaselessly churning world, a pre-adult world of Doritos and libidos, that the playwright seeks to lay bare." *–The NY Times* "STUPID KIDS [is] a sharp-edged ... whoosh of teen angst and conformity anguish. It is also very funny." *–NY Newsday* [2M, 2W] ISBN: 0-8222-1698-1

★ **COLLECTED STORIES by Donald Margulies.** From Obie Award-winner Donald Margulies comes a provocative analysis of a student-teacher relationship that turns sour when the protégé becomes a rival. "With his fine ear for detail, Margulies creates an authentic, insular world, and he gives equal weight to the opposing viewpoints of two formidable characters." *–The LA Times* "This is probably Margulies' best play to date ..." *–The NY Post* "... always fluid and lively, the play is thick with ideas, like a stock-pot of good stew." *–The Village Voice* [2W] ISBN: 0-8222-1640-X

★ **FREEDOMLAND by Amy Freed.** An overdue showdown between a son and his father sets off fireworks that illuminate the neurosis, rage and anxiety of one family – and of America at the turn of the millennium. "FREEDOMLAND's more obvious links are to *Buried Child* and *Bosoms and Neglect*. Freed, like Guare, is an inspired wordsmith with a gift for surreal touches in situations grounded in familiar and real territory." *–Curtain Up* [3M, 4W] ISBN: 0-8222-1719-8

★ **STOP KISS by Diana Son.** A poignant and funny play about the ways, both sudden and slow, that lives can change irrevocably. "There's so much that is vital and exciting about STOP KISS ... you want to embrace this young author and cheer her onto other works ... the writing on display here is funny and credible ... you also will be charmed by its heartfelt characters and up-to-the-minute humor." *–The NY Daily News* "... irresistibly exciting ... a sweet, sad, and enchantingly sincere play." *–The NY Times* [3M, 3W] ISBN: 0-8222-1731-7

★ **THREE DAYS OF RAIN by Richard Greenberg.** The sins of fathers and mothers make for a bittersweet elegy in this poignant and revealing drama. "... a work so perfectly judged it heralds the arrival of a major playwright ... Greenberg is extraordinary." *–The NY Daily News* "Greenberg's play is filled with graceful passages that are by turns melancholy, harrowing, and often, quite funny." *–Variety* [2M, 1W] ISBN: 0-8222-1676-0

★ **THE WEIR by Conor McPherson.** In a bar in rural Ireland, the local men swap spooky stories in an attempt to impress a young woman from Dublin who recently moved into a nearby "haunted" house. However, the tables are soon turned when she spins a yarn of her own. "You shed all sense of time at this beautiful and devious new play." *–The NY Times* "Sheer theatrical magic. I have rarely been so convinced that I have just seen a modern classic. Tremendous." *–The London Daily Telegraph* [4M, 1W] ISBN: 0-8222-1706-6

DRAMATISTS PLAY SERVICE, INC.
440 Park Avenue South, New York, NY 10016 212-683-8960 Fax 212-213-1539
postmaster@dramatists.com   www.dramatists.com